BURGERS

BURGERS

From Barbecue Ranch Burger to Miso Salmon Burger

PAUL GAYLER

PHOTOGRAPHY BY GUS FILGATE

GEORGETOWN
PUBLICATIONS

GEORGETOWN
PUBLICATIONS

This edition first published in Canada in 2005 by
Georgetown Publications Inc.

579 Richmond Street West, Suite 100
Toronto, Ontario CANADA
M5V 1Y6

Publisher Jacqui Small
Editor Madeline Weston
Art Director Lawrence Morton
Food stylist Linda Tubby
Props stylist Roisin Nield
Production Peter Colley

Library and Archives Canada Cataloguing
in Publication
Gayler, Paul
Burgers : from barbecue ranch burger to
miso salmon
burger / written by Paul Gayler.
Includes index.
ISBN 0-9735339-7-8
1. Cookery (Meat) 2. Hamburgers.
I. Title.
TX749.G39 2005   641.6'6
C2004-905245-4

Printed in Singapore

All recipes serve 4 unless otherwise stated.

Contents

You can't beat a good burger, that's why they're loved the world over. As with all brilliant ideas, the burger's appeal lies in its simplicity. What could be simpler than pressing together some good minced beef with a little seasoning, then grilling it and serving it in a bun, with pickles, ketchup, mustard, whatever takes your fancy? A well-dressed burger makes the perfect meal: nutritious and filling, with a combination of sweet/salt/sour flavours to tantalise the taste buds. What's more, it's quick to make, comforting to eat, and can be held in your hands.

The fast-food companies were quick to claim the burger as their own, but the qualities that make it suitable for mass production also make it perfect for cooking at home. So give it a go! In this book you will find over sixty recipes for burgers, ranging from the traditional beef versions such as the Classic all-American, to a Greek Souvlaki Burger, a Mediterranean Swordfish Burger and a Middle Eastern-inspired Pumpkin Couscous Burger, plus some exciting ideas for relishes and accompaniments. None of them is difficult or time consuming, and all of them will tempt you to make burgers the centrepiece of your meal, whether it's a summer barbecue, a quick midweek family supper or a celebration dinner (Fillet Burger Rossini with Foie Gras and Truffle Glaze would be perfect). Some of the burgers are designed for serving as pre-dinner nibbles with drinks: the Thai Lobster and Lemongrass Sticks, Peking Duck Wraps and the Trattoria Burger, but all the other burgers can be scaled down to serve in this way, too.

Chefs everywhere are rediscovering the burger. I hope this book will encourage you to do the same, and to restore the burger to its rightful place at the heart of the family kitchen.

The history of the burger

For people all over the world, the hamburger has come to represent modern American culture, yet this fast-food icon has a surprisingly long history, with roots buried deep in northern Europe.

Mincing beef to make it easier to eat is not a recent idea. In medieval Russia, tribes known as Tartars used to shred beef and eat it raw, hence steak tartare. German soldiers picked up the idea in the fourteenth century and took it back to their homeland, where the meat was flavoured with spices and herbs and eaten raw or cooked. This eventually became known as Hamburg steak, after the German city, and crossed the Atlantic with German immigrants in the nineteenth century. The term 'hamburger' appeared on a menu at Delmonico's restaurant in New York as early as 1834, and by the 1890s it was common across the United States. In the early days, Hamburg steak was a piece of beef that had been pounded to make it more tender, not minced, but by 1902 there were recipes in cookery books that included instructions to mince the meat and mix it with seasonings. The hamburger made its big leap to immortality when someone had the idea of serving it in a bun. Suddenly, it was portable, convenient and, thanks to the various toppings and the bread that soaked up the juices, ten times as delicious. The question is, who thought of it first? Several places in the United States claim to be the birthplace of the modern hamburger. Seymour, Wisconsin, has built a Hamburger Hall of Fame to back up its story that Charlie Nagreen, aged fifteen, was the first person ever to serve hamburgers, at the Outgamie County Fair in 1885. At Hamburg, New York, the legend goes that the Menches brothers substituted minced beef for pork in their famous sausage sandwiches, which they sold from a stand at a county fair there in 1885, and renamed them hamburgers. But what isn't in any doubt, since it was written up by a reporter from the New York Tribune, is that beef patties in a bun, called hamburgers, were on sale at the St Louis World's Fair in 1904. It seems that the vendor was Fletcher Davis, who had already built up quite a reputation in his hometown of Athens, Texas, for his toasted steak sandwiches. The term hamburger became shortened to burger, opening up the way for cheeseburgers and more modern inventions, such as tuna burgers, veggie burgers and chicken burgers. The early twentieth century was a time of rapid change in American society. As cars became affordable and better roads were built, the population became increasingly mobile. This new freedom opened up a new way of eating, too, one that meant you didn't even have to get out of your car. Drive-in restaurants, selling barbecued meats, hamburgers and hot dogs, became popular places for young people to hang out. Two brothers, Richard and Maurice McDonald, opened their McDonald Brothers Burger Bar Drive-in in 1940. Despite its success, they became tired of their teenage customers, and decided to open a new kind of restaurant where entire families could come and eat cheaply. The only food on sale was to be burgers; paper plates, cups and bags were to be used; and a factory production-line system in the kitchen meant that service was ultra-quick. Soon people were queuing round the block for the cheapest burgers in town, and the concept of fast food was born.

Now the hamburger is almost entirely associated with fast-food restaurants. It is the all-time American favourite, with nearly 5.5 billion burgers sold each year in the United States alone, meaning that the average American eats three a week. Yet familiarity has bred contempt. As the hamburger's popularity grew, unscrupulous operators sprang up who squeezed as much profit as they could out of inferior beef and damp, tasteless buns. From being a quick, nutritious snack, the hamburger came to symbolise for some the worst excesses of fast-food culture.

This book isn't about fast food, however. It's a celebration of what made the burger great in the first place. A well-made burger transcends the sum of its parts to become truly sublime. This is a fact that many talented chefs are aware of, which is why the burger has undergone something of a revival recently and now appears on some of the classiest restaurant menus in America. It may be the all-American classic; it may be a chef's flight of fancy, sandwiched between two halves of a bun, a crisp baguette or a light, fluffy focaccia; tuna, lobster, lamb, venison, roasted vegetables, goat's cheese, you name it. Yet all these burgers have something in common with the original: they are made from a very few quality ingredients, cooked quickly, and served up as fresh as can be. Now more than ever, the burger offers us the kind of food we want to eat. Its timeless appeal ensures that one hundred years after its first documented appearance at the St Louis World's Fair, the hamburger endures as not just America's but the world's most popular food.

How to make a burger

Burgers are so quick to make at home that once you get in the habit you might wonder why you ever bothered to buy them. Making them yourself means that you can control the quality of the meat and customise the flavourings to your own taste. When you've mastered the classic hamburger, move on to other meats (lamb in particular makes a great burger), game, fish and seafood, even vegetables, grains and beans. And have fun with the accompaniments – there's a big selection to choose from. Below are a few guidelines to ensure that your burgers always turn out the best:

Meat

Choosing meat: Because burgers are cooked for just a short time and contain only a few flavourings, the flavour of the meat shines through. This means that the better the meat, the better your burgers will taste. There's no need to buy expensive cuts, though. Instead, go for skirt, shin or chuck when making beefburgers. For lamb or pork, shoulder or leg is fine. Avoid packs of mince, as they tend to be wet and flavourless. For a juicy, succulent burger, you need to use meat that is about 20 per cent fat. This drains off during cooking but ensures that the burger remains moist, effectively basting it as it cooks. Over-lean meat can result in a dry, tough burger. Game makes excellent burgers. Meats such as pheasant and ostrich are well flavoured and nutritious. Because they are so lean, add a little fat to the mixture in the form of pork.

Preparing meat: The meat should be coarsely minced, if it is too finely minced, the burger is more likely to fall apart and the texture is less satisfying. Additions, such as garlic or chillies, should be chopped very finely. Most butchers mince their meat on a fine or medium setting, so you may have to ask for it to be prepared for you. Alternatively, mince it yourself at home, trimming it first. An old-fashioned hand-cranked mincer is surprisingly satisfying to use. You could use a food processor, but it's quite hard to get the right texture with it. Chop the meat into small cubes first with a large, sharp knife, then pulse it in the machine, being careful not to let it turn into a paste.

Making the burgers: Always chill the meat well before use; this helps the ingredients cohere when you mix them together. Then combine all the ingredients as quickly and lightly as possible, otherwise the burgers will be dense and heavy. Meats such as chicken can be pulsed briefly with all the flavourings in a food processor, but for most meats, once they are minced it's best to mix everything together with your hands in a large bowl. Use wet hands to shape the burgers, so the mixture doesn't stick to them. Don't squeeze the mixture into shape; just press it lightly together until it forms a ball. Then flatten it gently with the palm of your hand and neaten the edges so they don't fray. Make sure the burgers are an even thickness (about 2.5cm), so they cook evenly. Once you have shaped the burgers, place them on a baking tray and chill again, to firm up the meat before cooking.

Fish

When you are making fish burgers, buy very fresh fish fillets, remove the skin and check the flesh carefully for bones. Chill well. The fish is then usually finely chopped by hand and mixed with the other ingredients, or whizzed to a coarse paste in a food processor, depending on the desired texture. Fish can give off liquid sometimes, especially if the recipe requires you to marinate it, so drain this off before dividing the mixture into burgers. Shape as for meat and chill until firm. Cooking fish burgers requires care, so follow the instructions on the following page.

Vegetables

Making vegetarian burgers gives you a chance to be really inventive: lentils, nuts, grains such as millet and buckwheat, even cottage cheese and goat's cheese all make fantastic burgers. The secret is to get the mixture the right consistency so it will hold together during cooking. Ground nuts, breadcrumbs and egg are all useful for binding the mixture. Whizzing everything together in a blender or food processor is a quick method of mixing, and you can then shape and chill your burgers as for meat, above. Vegetarian burgers are not only for vegetarians!

Basic methods of cooking

There's no denying that burgers taste best when cooked on a chargrill. They must be the ultimate barbecue food, grilled over glowing coals, then slapped into a lightly toasted bun with the accompaniments of your choice and devoured straight away. Burgers such as vegetable and fish, however, can be too delicate for the chargrill, and are better fried in a little oil. However you cook your burgers, it rarely takes more than 10 minutes. No wonder they're everyone's favourite fast food!

Barbecuing

The secret of cooking on a barbecue is to wait until the flames have died down and you are left with glowing, reddish-grey embers. This generally means lighting the barbecue at least 40 minutes before you want to start cooking. Burgers are best cooked over a medium-high heat, i. e. when the red-hot coals are covered with a layer of white ash.

When the barbecue has reached the right temperature, brush the burgers with a little oil and put them on the grill: a heavy-duty one with fairly thick bars will minimise sticking. Resist the temptation to move them about or try to turn them until they are nicely charred underneath, otherwise they will stick.

Once a crust has formed, you should be able to release the burger from the bars of the grill and flip it over with a metal spatula to brown the other side. Besides making burgers easier to turn, searing the surface in this way also makes them more appetising, the lightly charred surface contains all those wonderful caramelised flavours that make chargrilled food so irresistible.

There's no need to press down on the burgers with a spatula to speed up cooking, if you do this, the precious juices will be lost and the burgers will be dry.

Cook the burgers according to taste: if you like them rare, test by pressing the centre gently with a finger, it should feel soft and yielding. The firmer it is, the more cooked it will be. Pork and chicken should always be cooked right through.

Frying

If you find a ridged grill pan difficult, and some burgers can have a tendency to stick or break up on them, it's fine to use a frying pan instead. This method is recommended for delicate burgers such as chicken and fish. Choose a nonstick frying pan with a heavy base so it will conduct the heat evenly. Heat a thin film of oil in it until almost smoking hot (for meat burgers) or until moderately hot (for fish and vegetable burgers), then add the burgers and cook until well coloured underneath. Turn with a spatula and cook the other side. Be careful not to overcrowd the pan, or the burgers will steam instead of fry. Except for tuna, which can be served rare like beef, fish burgers should be cooked all the way through, and should be golden on the outside, or at the most just lightly charred. For vegetable burgers, which are generally made from pre-cooked ingredients, all you need to do is ensure that they form a good golden crust on the outside and heat through thoroughly in the centre. A couple of the vegetable burgers in this book are deep-fried. Immersing them in hot oil like this gives them a wonderful, crisp crust and a contrasting soft centre. Heat the oil to 180°C in a deep-fat fryer or a deep saucepan and fry the burgers a few at a time. Drain on kitchen paper to remove excess fat before serving.

Grilling

For grilling burgers indoors, a ridged cast-iron grill pan is invaluable. Not only does it give food a hint of the smoky flavour that you get on an outdoor barbecue but the ridges mean that the fat drains away, making it a healthy cooking method. Choose a large one that goes across two rings on your hob, so you can cook a decent batch of burgers in one go. Before cooking, leave the grill pan over a medium-high heat until it is almost smoking hot (a good way of testing it is to throw a drop or two of water on to it; if it sizzles, the grill is hot enough). Then brush the burgers lightly with oil and proceed as above.

You can also cook burgers under an eye-level grill, although – because they don't have direct contact with the heat – they will lack that smoky flavour.

The ultimate burger with 'the works'

CLASSIC BEEF

The ultimate burger with 'the works'

800g good quality, coarsely minced beef, chilled
½ onion, finely chopped
½ garlic clove, crushed
1 tbsp chopped fresh flat-leaf parsley
½ tsp Dijon mustard
½ tbsp Worcestershire sauce
1 egg yolk
salt and freshly ground black pepper
vegetable or sunflower oil for cooking

TO SERVE · 4 BURGER BAPS, HALVED, TOASTED

'THE WORKS' · HORSERADISH AND SOUR CREAM CHIVE SAUCE
· TABASCO–CUMIN KETCHUP (SEE PAGE 125) · SWEET PICKLED DILL GHERKINS
· DICED AVOCADO · RED ONION RINGS · DIJON MUSTARD AIOLI

1 Place the chilled meat in a large bowl; add the onion, garlic, parsley, mustard and Worcestershire sauce.
2 Add the egg yolk and seasoning and mix thoroughly. Leave in the refrigerator for 1 hour.
3 Using wet hands, shape into 4 evenly sized burgers.
4 Heat a chargrill or pan grill until smoking hot.
5 Brush the burgers with a little oil, place on the grill and cook for 3–4 minutes on each side, until well browned, but still pink in the centre.
6 Serve the burgers in the toasted baps, spread and garnished with your choice of 'the works'.

Horseradish and sour cream chive sauce
100ml sour cream
1 tbsp creamed horseradish relish
1 tbsp chopped fresh chives
· Whisk the ingredients together and serve.

Dijon mustard aioli
100ml aioli (see page 126)
1 tsp Dijon mustard
salt and freshly ground black pepper
· Whisk the ingredients together and serve.

Classic all-American burger

800g well trimmed, coarsely minced beef, chilled
1 onion, finely chopped
salt and freshly ground black pepper
vegetable or sunflower oil for cooking
8 slices American style cheese
75g iceberg lettuce leaves, shredded
2 beef tomatoes, thickly sliced
1 onion, sliced

1 Mix the meat and the onion in a large bowl, season with salt, plenty of black pepper, and chill for 1 hour.
2 Divide the mix into 4 x 200g evenly sized burgers, and brush liberally all over with the oil.
3 Heat a chargrill or pan grill until very hot, add the burgers and cook for 3–4 minutes on each side, until cooked and slightly charred all over.
4 Preheat grill to its highest setting.
5 Place the burgers on a grill rack and cover with the cheese slices, place under the grill until melted.
6 Toast the baps, brush the bases with mustard and the lids with the mayonnaise.
7 Top the base of the baps with the shredded iceberg, followed by the burger, then by the onion and tomato slices. Finally, top with the sliced dill pickles, and replace the bap lids.
8 Serve with the ultimate fries, and lots of tomato ketchup.

TO SERVE · 4 BURGER BAPS, SPLIT · 30ML MILD AMERICAN MUSTARD · 60ML GOOD QUALITY MAYONNAISE · 2 SWEET DILL PICKLES, SLICED · THE ULTIMATE FRIES (SEE PAGE 139) · SIMPLE TOMATO KETCHUP (SEE PAGE 125), OR STORE BOUGHT

Blackened burger with grilled onion salad and yellow pico de gallo

Traditional Cajun style burgers from America's Deep South are always preferred well dressed and well seasoned; here they are unusually served on a warm French baguette, which I think is delicious. Although not normally served with a pico de gallo, I love this Mexican-style relish, it is cool and offsets the spicy burger beautifully.

vegetable or sunflower oil for cooking
1 onion
1 garlic clove, crushed
150g smoked sausage of your choice, such as chorizo, cut into 0.5cm dice
600g well trimmed, coarsely minced beef
¼ tsp dried thyme
¼ tsp dried oregano
¼ tsp ground cumin
⅛ tsp chilli powder
salt and freshly ground black pepper

1 Heat a small frying pan, and add a thin film of the oil to the pan; add the onion, garlic and sausage and fry until softened and lightly golden. Transfer to a large bowl, and allow to cool.

2 Add the minced beef, dried herbs and spices and mix together thoroughly; season with salt and pepper and chill for 1 hour.

3 Divide into 4 evenly sized burgers, and brush liberally with the oil.

4 Heat a chargrill or pan grill until very hot and add the burgers. Cook for 3–4 minutes on each side or longer if you prefer.

5 Halve the baguette, dress the bases with a spread of chilli mayo, topped with shredded iceberg lettuce. Top with the grilled onion salad, a burger, and finally a good spoonful of the yellow pico de gallo.

6 Close the burgers and serve.

Grilled onion salad

1 large or 2 small red onions,
  unpeeled
100ml olive oil
2 tbsp roughly chopped fresh
  coriander
juice of ½ lemon
splash of balsamic vinegar
salt and freshly ground black
  pepper

• Cut the onion across into 4 thick
slices, about 2cm thick, keeping
the skins on each slice.
• Heat a chargrill or pan grill until
hot. Brush the onion slices liberally
all over both sides with half the oil.
• Place the onions on the grill and
cook until almost charred brown,
but not burnt. Brush with more oil
during cooking if needed.
• Carefully using a fish slice,
remove the onions from the grill
and transfer to a shallow tray.
Discard the outer skin.
• Mix the remaining oil, chopped
coriander, lemon juice and a splash
of balsamic vinegar in a bowl, and
brush over the warm onions;
season to taste and keep warm.

TO SERVE • 4 X 12.5CM LENGTHS WARM BAGUETTE OR BAPS • CHILLI MAYO (SEE PAGE 126)
• 50G SHREDDED ICEBURG LETTUCE • GRILLED ONION SALAD • YELLOW PICO DE GALLO (SEE PAGE 128)

Open-faced Roquefort burger

100g Roquefort cheese, crumbled
200g unsalted butter, softened
2 tbsp snipped fresh chives
750g good quality, coarsely minced beef,
  well chilled
1 onion, finely chopped
1 tsp Dijon mustard
1 tsp Worcestershire sauce
2 egg yolks
1 garlic clove, crushed
salt and freshly ground black pepper
vegetable or sunflower oil for cooking

1 In a bowl, mix together the cheese with the butter and snipped chives.
2 Cut a sheet of greaseproof paper approximately 25 x 25cm. Mould the prepared butter in a strip about 4cm wide along the front edge of the paper then roll up tightly, twisting the ends to form a fat bonbon shape. Place the cheese roll in the freezer overnight.
3 In a large bowl, mix the remaining ingredients, then divide the hamburger mix into 8 evenly sized patties.
4 Remove the cheese roll from the freezer, allow to soften slightly and cut into 4 equal slices.
5 Place a slice of cheese roll on 4 of the patties and use the remaining 4 patties as lids; with your fingertips, pinch the edges together to seal in the cheese filling. Brush the burgers with a little oil.
6 Heat the grill and, when smoking hot, cook the burgers for 4–5 minutes on each side.
7 To serve, top each section of the baguette with a sliced tomato, then a grilled burger and top with some dressed salad leaves, and serve.

TO SERVE · 4 X 12.5cm LENGTHS FRENCH BAGUETTE · 8 TOMATOES, SLICED · 75G ROCKET LEAVES · 4 TBSP FRENCH DRESSING OF YOUR CHOICE

Bymark hamburger
Sirloin burger with porcini mushrooms, Brie de Meaux and truffle aioli

This wonderful recipe comes courtesy of top Canadian chef Mark McEwan, of Toronto's trendy North 44 Restaurant. The melting Brie and fat juicy porcini mushrooms work brilliantly together while the truffle aioli adds a touch of elegance.

800g trimmed beef striploin, hand chopped
salt and freshly ground black pepper
olive oil for cooking
4 fresh porcini mushrooms, sliced 1cm thick
4 slices Brie de Meaux cheese

Truffle aioli
120ml good quality mayonnaise
1 tbsp lemon juice
2 tsp truffle oil or paste
• Whisk the ingredients together and serve.

1 Place the chopped striploin in a bowl, season liberally with salt and pepper.
2 Form into 2.5cm thick patties, then brush lightly with olive oil.
3 Heat a chargrill or pan grill until very hot, add the burgers and grill until desired doneness (about 4 minutes per side for rare), remove.
4 Brush the sliced porcini mushrooms with the olive oil and grill until tender, season with salt and pepper.
5 Finally, grill the baps until golden.
6 Top each burger with a slice of Brie de Meaux cheese.
7 Place the mushrooms on each burger bap base, then top with the burger and cheese slice.
8 Finally spoon over a little truffle aioli, close the burger with its lid and serve.

TO SERVE • 4 BURGER BAPS, SPLIT • TRUFFLE AIOLI

Ploughman's burger with two cheeses, balsamic onion pickle and classic coleslaw

15g unsalted butter

1 onion, finely chopped

1 garlic clove, crushed

½ tsp smoked paprika

1 tsp picked fresh thyme leaves

800g well trimmed, coarsely minced beef, chilled

2 tbsp barbecue sauce

2 tbsp chopped fresh flat-leaf parsley

2 egg yolks

salt and freshly ground black pepper

40g grated cheddar cheese

vegetable or sunflower oil for cooking

1 Heat the butter in a frying pan, add the onion, garlic, smoked paprika and thyme. Cook for 1–2 minutes until the onions are softened but not coloured. Place in a bowl to cool.

2 Add the chilled meat, barbecue sauce, parsley and egg yolks, and season to taste. Carefully bring the mix together, making sure not to overwork it or it will become tough. Chill in the refrigerator for 1 hour.

3 Divide the mix into 4 x 200g evenly sized burgers.

4 With a wet thumb, make an indent into the top of each burger. Fill the indent in each burger with cheddar cheese then fold up the side to secure the cheese in the centre. Brush liberally with the oil.

5 Heat a chargrill or pan grill until very hot, add the burgers and cook for 3–4 minutes on each side or longer if you prefer.

6 Place a good dollop of the onion pickle on the base of each roll, then top with a slice of Emmental cheese and some sliced tomatoes.

7 Place the burger on top, followed by the coleslaw. Replace the lid and serve with the shredded iceberg lettuce and extra pickle. Jacket potatoes oozing with lots of butter would be great too!

TO SERVE · 4 LARGE CRUSTY ROLLS OR CIABATTAS, SPLIT · 4 SLICES EMMENTAL CHEESE · 2 BEEF TOMATOES, THINLY SLICED · CLASSIC COLESLAW (SEE PAGE 133) · 50G SHREDDED ICEBERG LETTUCE · BALSAMIC ONION PICKLE (SEE PAGE 130)

Bloody Mary burger with celeriac Waldorf and Tabasco–cumin ketchup

800g well trimmed, coarsely minced beef
1 onion, peeled, finely chopped
1 stick celery, peeled, finely chopped
2 tbsp tomato ketchup
1 tbsp horseradish relish
1 tbsp Worcestershire sauce
1 tbsp chopped fresh flat-leaf parsley
salt and freshly ground black pepper
vegetable or sunflower oil for cooking

1 Place the meat in a large bowl and add the onion, celery, ketchup, horseradish, Worcestershire sauce and parsley. Season with salt and pepper. Mix well but do not overwork, then chill for 1 hour.
2 Divide the mix into 4 evenly sized burgers and brush liberally with oil.
3 Heat a chargrill or pan grill until hot, add the burgers and cook for 5–6 minutes.
4 Toast the baps, top with shredded cos gem, then a heap of celeriac Waldorf.
5 Place a burger on top, and drizzle some Tabasco–cumin ketchup over; close the bap.
6 Serve with some extra ketchup alongside and oven cheese fries. A tall glass of Bloody Mary served alongside is a welcome addition.

Celeriac Waldorf

1 celeriac, peeled
1 Granny Smith apple, peeled and cored
75ml good quality crème fraîche
½ tsp Dijon mustard
2 tbsp soaked raisins
salt and freshly ground black pepper

• Cut the celeriac and apple into small matchstick size pieces, either by hand or with a kitchen mandolin.
• Place in a bowl, add the crème fraîche, mustard and raisins; mix well and season to taste.

TO SERVE • 4 SESAME BURGER BAPS, SPLIT • COS GEM LETTUCE LEAVES, SHREDDED
• CELERIAC WALDORF • TABASCO–CUMIN KETCHUP (SEE PAGE 125) • OVEN CHEESE FRIES (SEE PAGE 139)

New Mexican burger with smoky guacamole amd sweet potato mole

In this Mexican inspired burger I replace the soft bap with a
crispy fried corn tortilla shell that adds an interesting contrast of texture.

600g good quality, coarsely minced beef, well chilled
1 onion, finely chopped
2 garlic cloves, crushed
2 small red chillies, deeseeded, finely chopped
1 tsp smoked paprika
1 tsp ground cumin
3 tbsp chopped fresh coriander
salt

1 In a large bowl, mix all the ingredients together and chill for up to 1 hour.
   Shape into 4 evenly sized burgers, brush with oil and grill, or fry in a
   nonstick pan over moderate heat, for 4–5 minutes each side, until cooked.
2 To serve, arrange 4 tortilla shells on individual serving plates, place a few
   salad leaves on each shell and top with a dollop of sweet potato mole.
3 Arrange a burger on top and spoon the smoky guacamole over. Garnish
   with a dollop of sour cream and some coriander leaves and
   serve with lime wedges.

Sweet potato mole

200g canned tomatoes, chopped
1 red pepper, deseeded, chopped
1 onion, finely chopped
1 garlic clove, crushed
1 tbsp brown sugar
1 corn tortilla, chopped
1 tbsp hot Mexican pepper sauce
1 tbsp sesame seeds, toasted
⅛ tsp each ground cinnamon,
   ground cumin, ground coriander,
   and ground cloves
1 tbsp each chopped fresh
   oregano and coriander
125g peanut butter
1 orange sweet potato, peeled, cut
   into 1cm cubes
salt and freshly ground black
   pepper

• Place the chopped tomatoes, red
pepper, onion, garlic, brown sugar,
tortilla, chilli sauce, sesame seeds,
and herbs and spices in a saucepan,
cover with 150ml of water, bring to
the boil over a high heat.
• Cook for 10 minutes; reduce the
heat and simmer for a further
30 minutes or until the mixture is
thick and aromatic.
• Place in a blender and whiz to a
smooth purée. Return to the pan.
• Add the peanut butter and heat,
stirring, until smooth.
• Add the cubed sweet potato and
cook for 10–15 minutes until the
potato is just cooked; adjust the
seasoning before serving.

TO SERVE • 4 CRISPY FRIED CORN TORTILLAS • GREEN SALAD LEAVES • SWEET POTATO MOLE
• SMOKY GUACAMOLE • 60ML SOUR CREAM • FRESH CORIANDER LEAVES • 1 LIME CUT INTO WEDGES

Smoky guacamole

1 ripe but firm avocado, peeled, stoned
4 tbsp olive oil
4 ripe but firm tomatoes, cut into
  0.5cm dice
½ red onion, chopped
2 spring onions, chopped
1 green jalepeño chilli, deseeded, finely
  chopped
juice of 1 lime
pinch of sugar, pinch of ground cumin
3 tbsp chopped fresh coriander
salt and freshly ground black pepper

• Heat a chargrill or pan grill until hot.
• Brush the avocado halves all over liberally
with 1 tbsp of the oil; place on the grill and
cook until lightly golden but not charred
(which will make the flavour bitter), remove
and allow to cool.
• Place the avocado in a bowl and mash
lightly with a fork; add the tomatoes, red
onion, spring onions and chilli.
• Add the lime juice, sugar, ground cumin and
coriander, and lastly the remaining oil. Adjust
the seasoning and set aside.

Steak tartare burger with herb-mustard and blue-cheese aioli, and matchstick fries

800g well trimmed, coarsely minced beef, chilled

2 small shallots, finely chopped

2 tbsp chopped fresh parsley

6 cocktail gherkins, rinsed, dried, finely chopped

2 tbsp superfine capers, rinsed, finely chopped

2 egg yolks

salt and freshly ground black pepper

vegetable or sunflower oil for cooking

1 Place the meat in a large bowl, add the shallots, parsley, gherkins and capers. Beat in the egg yolks and season with salt and pepper; do not overwork the mix.

2 Leave in the refrigerator for 1 hour before use.

3 Divide the mix, using wet hands, into 4 x 200g evenly sized burgers.

4 Heat a chargrill or pan grill until very hot. Brush the burgers liberally all over with the oil.

5 Place on the grill, and cook for 3–4 minutes on each side until cooked.

6 Toast the burger baps; cover the bases with the sliced tomatoes, watercress, then the burgers.

7 Spoon the herb-mustard and blue-cheese aioli over and cover with the top lid.

8 Serve with matchstick fries.

Herb-mustard and blue-cheese aioli

2 tbsp herb mustard

100ml basic mayonnaise (see page 126)

1 garlic clove, crushed

2 tbsp chopped fresh chives

75g of your favourite blue cheese (e.g. Stilton, Gorgonzola, Roquefort), crumbled

salt and freshly ground black pepper

• In a bowl, blend together the mustard, mayonnaise, garlic and chives; fold in the crumbled cheese, blend well and season to taste.

TO SERVE • 4 BURGER BAPS, SPLIT • 2 BEEF TOMATOES, THINLY SLICED • 50G WATERCRESS • HERB-MUSTARD AND BLUE-CHEESE AIOLI • MATCHSTICK FRIES (SEE PAGE 139)

Barbecued oyster burger with blue-cheese sauce, and bacon, spinach and red onion salad

700g well trimmed, coarsely minced beef, chilled
1 onion, finely chopped
1 tbsp chopped fresh flat-leaf parsley
1 tbsp horseradish relish
1 tsp tomato ketchup
1 egg, lightly beaten
salt and freshly ground black pepper
4 large freshly shucked oysters
vegetable or sunflower oil for cooking

1 Place the beef in a bowl, add the onion and parsley, and mix well. Add the horseradish, ketchup and egg and mix well together; season to taste. Cover, then refrigerate for 1 hour. Using wet hands, divide the mix into 4 evenly sized portions.

2 Shape each into a ball then, with wet fingers, make a deep indentation into the ball. Place 1 oyster into the hole, then seal up again to secure the oyster within. Flatten slightly into burgers, then brush liberally with oil and cook for 3–4 minutes each side, or a little longer if preferred.

3 Toast the brioche slices, top with the bacon, spinach and red onion salad, then top with the burgers. Drizzle the blue-cheese sauce over and serve with sweet potato fries.

Blue-cheese sauce

75ml double cream
1 tsp fresh thyme leaves
60ml chicken stock
1 tsp cornflour
50g blue cheese, crumbled
salt and freshly ground black pepper

• In a pan, place the cream, thyme, chicken stock and cornflour. Over a low heat, cook for 2 minutes; remove and allow to cool slightly.
• Add the blue cheese and blend until melted. Season to taste and serve warm.

TO SERVE · 4 SLICES BRIOCHE LOAF · BACON, SPINACH AND RED ONION SALAD (SEE PAGE 133) · BLUE-CHEESE SAUCE · SWEET POTATO FRIES (SEE PAGE 140)

Barbecue ranch burger

with smoky corn relish and chimichurri peppers

150g cooked red kidney beans
  (canned are fine)
650g well trimmed, coarsely minced beef
1 onion, finely chopped
1 garlic clove, crushed
1 tsp fresh thyme leaves
1 tsp Dijon mustard
60ml barbecue sauce (see page 125)
salt and freshly ground black pepper
vegetable or sunflower oil for cooking
4 wooden skewers

TO SERVE · 4 CHORIZO BURGER BAPS, SPLIT (SEE PAGE 135)
· CHIMICHURRI PEPPERS (SEE PAGE 129) · SMOKY CORN RELISH
(SEE PAGE 112) · SPICY RED-CHILLI ONION RINGS (SEE PAGE 140)

1 Place the beans in a bowl and crush them with a fork.
2 Add the remaining ingredients, except the oil, and work together to form a paste; do not overwork. Chill for 1 hour in the refrigerator.
3 Divide the mix into 4 evenly sized burgers and brush liberally with the oil.
4 Heat a chargrill or pan grill until hot, add the burgers and cook for 4–5 minutes until cooked.
5 Toast the baps; place the chimichurri peppers on the base baps, top each with a burger and add a dollop of corn relish on top. Close with the top of the baps.
6 Plunge a wooden skewer down through the centre of each burger bap, place the onion rings draped over the sticks and serve.

Barbecued hamburgers for a crowd (makes about 32 patties)

Eula Mae Doré has been cooking her Cajun specialities on Avery Island, Louisiana, for almost half a century. This recipe is for those not lucky enough to visit the Island to sample her home cooking! The Island has also been home to Tabasco sauce since 1868.

2.75kg ground beef
900g lean ground pork
100g freshly chopped yellow onions
1½ tbsp salt
1 tbsp cayenne
1 tbsp freshly ground black pepper
1 tbsp Tabasco sauce
2 tbsp Worcestershire sauce
100ml vegetable oil

1 Combine all the ingredients except the oil in a very large mixing bowl; mix well. Form into about 32 evenly sized patties and brush with the oil.
2 Heat a chargrill, pan grill or frying pan, and grill or fry to desired doneness.
3 More oil can be brushed on the patties while they cook.
4 Just before taking the patties off the heat, brush them liberally with Beb's barbecue sauce. Toast the small burger baps, place the burgers in them and serve.

TO SERVE · 32 SMALL BURGER BAPS
· 400ML BEB'S BARBECUE SAUCE (SEE PAGE 125)

Big Apple deli burger with Swiss cheese and barbecue coleslaw

100ml tomato juice

2 shallots, finely chopped

1 tbsp coriander seeds, toasted, crushed

¼ tsp cayenne pepper

½ tsp paprika

1 tbsp molasses or black treacle

800g well trimmed, coarsely minced beef, chilled

1 tbsp chopped fresh flat-leaf parsley

salt and freshly ground black pepper

1 Place the tomato juice, shallots, spices and molasses in a small pan and bring to the boil; cook for 1 minute, then remove and allow to cool.

2 Place the meat and parsley in a bowl, add the cooked sauce and mix well. Cover and place in the refrigerator for up to 1 hour.

3 Divide the mix into 4 x 200g evenly sized burgers and brush liberally with oil.

4 Heat a chargrill or pan grill until very hot. Place the burgers on the grill and cook for 3–4 minutes on each side.

5 Toast the baps, then lightly spread the base baps with mustard.

6 Top with a burger and a slice of Gruyère cheese, place under a hot grill to melt. Top with some sliced gherkin and the lettuce. Garnish with the barbecue coleslaw and serve. Baked jacket potatoes go particularly well with this burger.

TO SERVE · 4 RYE OR PLAIN BURGER BAPS, SPLIT · MUSTARD · 4 LETTUCE LEAVES · 2 DILL PICKLES, THINLY SLICED · 4 SLICES SWISS GRUYÈRE CHEESE · BARBECUE COLESLAW (SEE PAGE 133)

The Wolseley hamburger

Since the Wolseley restaurant opened its doors in autumn 2003, it has received many accolades for its simple, big-flavoured and down to earth cooking. Chef Chris Galvin, a great friend, is the main reason for its rapid rise to fame.

640g lean chuck steak, coarsely minced, chilled

160g beef fat, preferably from striploin, finely minced

salt and freshly ground black pepper

vegetable or sunflower oil for cooking

1 Place the steak and beef fat in a bowl along with a little seasoning. Bring the mix together, forming it lightly, just enough to hold. Do not overwork or the mix will become tough. Chill in the refrigerator for 1 hour before use.

2 Heat a chargrill or pan grill until very hot.

3 Divide the mix into 4 evenly sized burgers and brush liberally with oil.

4 Cook until desired degree, according to personal taste.

5 Toast the baps on the grill. Place the burgers on the bap bases, add a slice of onion, slice of tomato and finally slices of dill pickles. Top with the lid and serve.

Fritas with Cuban avocado salsa and tomato sofrito

Fritas is the name given to mini sized hamburgers, eaten on the go all over Cuba. They are sold by street vendors and they make the ideal snack food. I like to serve these burgers with spicy plantain chips, known affectionately as chilli willies! Allow two burgers per person.

125g fresh white breadcrumbs
100ml milk
600g well trimmed, coarsely minced beef
200g minced pork
1 egg, lightly beaten
1 onion, peeled, finely chopped
1 garlic clove, crushed
1 tbsp light soy sauce
2 tsp tomato ketchup
1 tsp Worcestershire sauce
pinch of paprika
salt and freshly ground black pepper
vegetable or sunflower oil for cooking

1 Soak the breadcrumbs in the milk for 5 minutes, or until all the liquid is absorbed. In a bowl gently combine both meats with the breadcrumbs. Add all the remaining ingredients, mix well together but do not overwork. Place in the refrigerator for 1 hour.

2 Divide the mix into 8 small, evenly sized burgers, brush liberally with the oil.

3 Heat a chargrill or pan grill until very hot, add the burgers and cook for 2–3 minutes on each side, or longer if preferred.

4 Toast the baps; top the bases with the shredded iceberg, followed by the salsa. Top each with a burger, then spoon some hot tomato sofrito over.

5 Replace the burger lids, serve with the spicy plantain chips and enjoy!

TO SERVE • 8 SMALL BURGER BAPS, SPLIT • 50G SHREDDED ICEBERG LETTUCE • CUBAN AVOCADO SALSA (SEE PAGE 131) • TOMATO SOFRITO • SPICY PLANTAIN CHIPS (SEE PAGE 140)

Tomato sofrito

30ml olive oil
1 onion, peeled, finely chopped
2 garlic cloves, crushed
½ tsp dried oregano
½ tsp ground cumin
2 tbsp hot pepper sauce
1 x 400g can peeled plum
   tomatoes or 500g fresh
   tomatoes, chopped
1 tbsp tomato purée
• Heat the olive oil in a pan, add
the onion, garlic, and dried
oregano; cook over a low heat
for 5–6 minutes until softened.
• Add the cumin, hot pepper
sauce and cook for a further
2 minutes.
• Add the chopped tomatoes,
tomato purée and cook for
10–15 minutes until all the
juices have evaporated and the
sofrito is thick in consistency.
This will keep, covered, in the
refrigerator for 2 weeks.

Rumpsteak burger with bacon brioche, and snail and parsley butter sauce

Richard Corrigan , chef-proprietor and talented chef of the Lindsay House in London has been cooking wonderful, inventive dishes like this for many years – to rave reviews.

600g well trimmed rump steak, chilled
80g beef bone marrow
15g unsalted butter
1 small onion, peeled, finely chopped
2 tsp chopped fresh marjoram leaves
salt and freshly ground black pepper
sunflower oil for cooking

1 Preheat the oven to 230°C/Gas 8.

2 Using a sharp knife, chop the meat until it has a very fine minced texture. Place in a bowl; grate the bone marrow directly into the bowl.

3 Heat the butter in a small pan and sweat the onion and marjoram until soft but not coloured. Cool slightly, then add to the meat in the bowl; season well.

4 Mix together with your hands without squeezing, then divide into 4 and shape each portion lightly into a thick patty, like a tournedos, about 2.5cm thick. Do not press together or the steak burgers will be tough.

5 Heat a film of oil in a frying pan with an ovenproof handle.

6 Sear and brown the burgers gently on both sides, then transfer the pan to the oven and finish cooking – 3 minutes for rare, 5 minutes for medium rare. Toast the brioche slices under a preheated grill.

7 Set each steak burger on a slice of brioche, and serve the snail and parsley butter sauce alongside, with the crispy potatoes cooked in duck fat.

TO SERVE · 4 SLICES BACON BRIOCHE · CRISPY POTATOES COOKED IN DUCK FAT · SNAIL AND PARSLEY BUTTER SAUCE

Snail and parsley butter sauce

2 tbsp olive oil
175g canned snails, drained, roughly chopped
1 garlic clove, crushed
3 egg yolks
150g good quality French unsalted butter, clarified
4 tbsp roughly chopped fresh flat-leaf parsley
salt and freshly ground black pepper
cayenne pepper
1 tsp lemon juice

• Heat a small frying pan with the oil until hot, add the snails and garlic and sauté for 2 minutes until lightly golden in colour, remove, keep warm.

• Place the egg yolks along with 1 tbsp of water in a heatproof bowl, and place above a pan of simmering water.

• Whisk vigorously until the egg thickens in volume and becomes light and fluffy. Remove the bowl from the pan, then gradually add the clarified butter to the eggs in a thin stream, until the mixture thickens (do not add too much butter at one go, or the mix will separate).

• When all the butter has been added, the mixture should be thick enough to coat the back of a spoon.

• Carefully add the snails and the parsley, season with salt and pepper, a little cayenne, and lemon juice; keep warm.

Crispy potatoes cooked in duck fat

4 medium-large baking potatoes, washed
60ml sunflower oil
30ml duck fat
coarse sea salt

• Preheat oven to 180°C/Gas 4.
• Place the potatoes on a baking tray and place in the preheated oven to cook for 1 hour; remove and cool slightly, cut in half lengthways.
• Using a large tablespoon, carefully remove the inner part, leaving the skin behind and keeping the inside of the potato intact.
• Cut the potatoes into thick wedges lengthways.
• Heat the oil and fat in a large nonstick frying pan, add the potatoes and cook until golden and crispy, turning them often for even colouring.
• Drain on kitchen paper; sprinkle with sea salt before serving.

Spiced Mediterranean burgers (serves 8)

Television celebrity chef and good friend Anthony Worrall Thompson is renowned for his passion for Mediterranean cuisine. This burger encapsulates it all – it is full of flavour, delicately spiced and wonderful cooked over a barbecue.

450g finely minced beef
450g finely minced lamb
½ onion, peeled, finely grated
1 tsp finely chopped garlic
1 tbsp extra-virgin olive oil
2 tbsp chopped fresh flat-leaf parsley
1 tbsp chopped fresh coriander
1 tsp dried oregano
½ tsp ground cinnamon
½ tsp ground cumin
1 tsp chilli sauce
salt and freshly ground black pepper

1 Preheat the barbecue or grill.
2 Place the burger ingredients in a large bowl, blend the mixture with your hands, taking care not to overwork it.
3 Form the mixture into 8 long oval shapes, about 2.5cm thick.
4 Chargrill, grill or fry the burgers for about 5 minutes on each side for rare, or to your taste.
5 Split the rolls or pitta breads without cutting them through. Remove some of the bread from the centre of the rolls. Place some tomato and shallot slices in the rolls, add the burgers, and garnish with flat-leaf parsley, fresh coriander and Greek yogurt.

TO SERVE · 8 SMALL BAGUETTE ROLLS/PITTA BREAD · 8 SHALLOTS, PEELED, THINLY SLICED · CHOPPED FRESH FLAT-LEAF PARSLEY · 4 BEEF TOMATOES, THINLY SLICED · 4 WHOLE FRESH CORIANDER LEAVES · 150ML PLAIN GREEK YOGURT

Beetroot burger

This Scandinavian-style burger recipe from friend Jill Dupleix is both tasty and unusual. A self taught cook, Jill became *The Times* cook in 2000, and is one of our best loved and respected food writers. This recipe comes from her book *Simple Food*.

1 tbsp unsalted butter
1 tbsp olive oil
1 onion, peeled, finely chopped
500g minced beef
2 egg yolks
1 tbsp capers, rinsed and chopped
sea salt and freshly ground black pepper
3 tbsp pickled beetroot, finely chopped
1 tbsp pickled beetroot juice
vegetable oil for cooking

1 Heat the butter and olive oil in a frying pan, and cook the onion slowly until pale and soft, then allow to cool.
2 Combine the minced beef, egg yolks, capers, sea salt and pepper.
3 Add the onion and mix thoroughly together.
4 Add the pickled beetroot and juice, mix well.
5 With wet hands, shape the mixture into 4 large flat burgers (the traditional shape), or make 8 smaller, taller patties.
6 Heat a chargrill or cast iron grill pan, oil it and the burgers lightly and cook them on a medium heat for about 5 minutes each side (alternatively heat a little oil in a frying pan and cook them).
7 Toast the muffins, serve the burgers on the toasted muffins with a little salad of tossed green leaves, or a little wilted spinach and small boiled new potatoes.

TO SERVE · 4 ENGLISH MUFFINS · SALAD OF TOSSED GREEN LEAVES OR WILTED SPINACH · SMALL BOILED NEW POTATOES

TO SERVE • 4 BURGER BAPS OR ENGLISH MUFFINS, SPLIT • CELERIAC RÉMOULADE (SEE PAGE 133) • 50G WATERCRESS • 90G FOIE GRAS, IN 4 SLICES • 8 SLICES FRESH TRUFFLE (OPTIONAL) • TRUFFLE GLAZE • MIXED LEAF SALAD • THE ULTIMATE FRIES (SEE PAGE 139)

Truffle glaze

1 tbsp honey
150ml medium sweet
  Madeira wine
1 tbsp Champagne vinegar
75ml olive oil
1 tbsp truffle oil or truffle
  paste
salt and freshly ground
  black pepper

• Place the honey and
Madeira in a small pan, bring
to the boil.

• Reduce the liquid down
until only 2 tbsp remain.

• Add the vinegar, then whisk
in the oils to form an
emulsion; season to taste.

Fillet burger rossini with foie gras, truffle glaze and celeriac rémoulade

This is a bit of a 'posh' burger! The ingredients may be more luxurious than most burger recipes, but it's a burger I would happily enjoy every day. You have to spoil yourself occasionally!

400g well trimmed, coarsely minced beef, chilled
½ tbsp picked thyme leaves
salt and freshly ground black pepper
vegetable or sunflower oil for cooking
4 x 120g fillet steaks

1 Mix the minced beef, thyme and seasoning in a bowl, cover and chill for 1 hour. Divide the mix into 4 small evenly sized burgers, brush liberally with oil.
2 Heat a chargrill or pan grill until very hot, add the burgers and small fillet steaks, and cook for 2–3 minutes on each side.
3 Toast the baps, place a good dollop of celeriac rémoulade on the bap bases, then top with the grilled fillet steaks, a little watercress, followed by the burgers. Heat a nonstick pan with no oil and, when very hot, sauté the foie gras for 30 seconds each side.
4 Place the foie gras on the burgers, top with the truffle slices, if using, and spoon the truffle glaze over. Serve with a mixed leaf salad and the ultimate fries alongside.

Trattoria burger on focaccia bianco, with white onion jam and salsa verde drizzle

Here a well-flavoured burger mix is thinly spread over the focaccia base, set on a bed of sweet onions,
and topped with a lively, tangy salsa verde. Cut into small squares it makes a wonderful canapé to serve with drinks.

250g well trimmed, coarsely minced beef

175g minced pork

1 onion, finely chopped

½ tsp ground cinnamon

1 tbsp fennel seeds, toasted

1 garlic clove, crushed

2 tbsp pine nuts, toasted

1 tbsp chopped fresh oregano

1 tbsp chopped fresh rosemary

2 tsp tomato purée

pinch of dried chilli flakes

salt and freshly ground black pepper

1 ball of buffalo mozzarella, grated

75g pecorino cheese, grated

olive oil for cooking

Salsa verde

1 garlic clove, crushed
2 tbsp chopped fresh flat-leaf parsley
2 tbsp chopped fresh basil leaves
1 tbsp superfine capers, rinsed and dried
salt and freshly ground black pepper
1 anchovy fillet, rinsed, chopped
¼ tsp Dijon mustard
1 tsp balsamic vinegar
100ml olive oil
• Place the garlic, herbs, capers, a little salt
in a mortar and pestle, crush to a coarse
paste; add the anchovy, mustard, vinegar
and crush again.
• Gradually add the oil to form a sauce,
adjust the seasoning and serve.

White onion jam

45ml olive oil
15g unsalted butter
2 onions peeled, thinly sliced
40g sugar
1 tsp picked fresh thyme leaves
100ml white wine vinegar
salt and freshly ground black pepper
• Heat the oil and butter in a pan, add
the onions, sugar and thyme; cook over a
low heat for 10–12 minutes until golden,
soft and caramelised.
• Add the vinegar, cook for a further
10 minutes until the onions take on a
sweet and sour flavour, remove, season
to taste and allow to go cold.

TO SERVE · 1 X RECIPE FOR FOCACCIA DOUGH (SEE PAGE 136)
· WHITE ONION JAM · SALSA VERDE

1 In a bowl, mix all the ingredients together except the mozzarella and percorino cheeses; season to taste, chill until needed.
2 Make the focaccia dough, following the recipe to the final stage, then roll it out to fit a shallow 20 x 25cm baking tin, about 0.5cm thick.
3 Cover the base liberally with the white onion jam, then spread the meat evenly over the onions, drizzle a little olive oil over.
4 Preheat the oven to 190°C/Gas 5.
5 Place the focaccia in the oven and bake for 15 minutes, then remove, sprinkle the grated cheeses over, and return to the oven for a further 10 minutes.
6 Remove and allow to cool before cutting into portions. Top each portion with a good drizzle of salsa verde before serving.

Tandoori lamb burger

MORE MEAT

Tandoori lamb burger with mint sambal and kachumbar piccalilli

800g well trimmed, coarsely minced lamb
1 onion, finely chopped
2 garlic cloves, crushed
2 tbsp natural yogurt
1 tbsp mango chutney
2.5cm piece root ginger, finely grated
1 tsp coriander seeds, crushed
1 tsp cumin seeds, crushed
½ tsp garam masala
¼ tsp turmeric
salt and freshly ground black pepper
pinch of cayenne
vegetable or sunflower oil for cooking

TO SERVE · 4 CUMIN NAAN BREADS,
WARMED · MINT SAMBAL · KACHUMBAR
PICCALILLI (SEE PAGE 128)

1 Place the lamb in a large bowl, add the onion, garlic and yogurt, cover and leave for 30 minutes in the refrigerator.
2 Add all the remaining ingredients, mixing well, then return to the refrigerator. Leave overnight for the best results.
3 Divide the mix into 8 equal portions, then using wet hands roll each of them into a long sausage shape, brush them liberally with the oil.
4 Heat a chargrill or pan grill until hot, add the burgers and cook for 5–6 minutes until cooked and lightly charred all over, turning them regularly.
5 Serve the burgers on the warm cumin naan breads, topped with the kachumbar piccalilli, and with the mint sambal alongside.

Mint sambal
75ml Greek yogurt
2 onions, peeled, finely chopped
¼ tsp garam masala
2.5cm piece root ginger, finely grated
1 garlic clove, crushed
50g mint leaves
· Place all the ingredients in a blender and whiz together; cover and chill for at least 2 hours, preferably overnight, before serving.

Souvlaki burger wraps with beetroot and horseradish tzatziki

800g well trimmed, coarsely minced lamb
50g crumbled feta cheese
1 onion, finely chopped
1 garlic clove, crushed
2 tbsp chopped fresh flat-leaf parsley
1 tbsp chopped fresh mint
2 tsp chopped fresh oregano
½ tsp ground cumin
salt and freshly ground black pepper
vegetable or sunflower oil for cooking
4 wooden skewers, soaked

1 Mix all the ingredients together for the burgers in a bowl, chill for 1 hour.
2 Using wet hands, mould the mix around 4 soaked and oiled wooden skewers in a sausage shape. Brush liberally with oil.
3 Heat a chargrill or pan grill until hot, add the skewers and cook for 4–5 minutes until cooked and lightly charred, turning them regularly. Remove and keep them warm.
4 Place the flatbreads on the grill and char lightly, about 30–40 seconds on each side.
5 Sprinkle some iceberg lettuce, red onion and parsley over the base of each grilled flatbread. Spoon some beetroot and horseradish tzatziki over, then finally remove the skewers from the burgers and place on each flatbread.
6 Roll up the flatbreads to enclose and eat immediately.

TO SERVE · 4 THIN MIDDLE EASTERN FLATBREADS · SHREDDED ICEBERG LETTUCE · 1 SMALL RED ONION, THINLY SLICED
· 50G ROUGHLY CHOPPED FLAT-LEAF PARSLEY · BEETROOT AND HORSERADISH TZATZIKI (SEE PAGE 128)

Souvlaki burger wraps

Sosatie burgers with peanut curry chiffonade, and apricot and red onion chutney

Traditionally sosaties are kebabs marinated in a thick, sweet curry sauce before being chargrilled over hot coals: a marrying of sweet and savoury flavours originally introduced from Malaysia. These burgers are based on this theme.

800g well trimmed, coarsely minced lamb
1 onion, grated
1 garlic clove, crushed
2 tbsp apricot jam
1 tbsp curry powder
1 tsp ground coriander
¼ tsp ground ginger
¼ tsp turmeric
½ tsp grated lemon zest
salt and freshly ground black pepper
pinch of dried chilli flakes
vegetable or sunflower oil for cooking
4 wooden skewers, soaked

1 Place the lamb in a large bowl, add all the remaining burger ingredients and work together; do not overwork or the mix will toughen. Chill in the refrigerator for 1 hour.
2 Divide the mix into 12 small evenly sized balls then, with wet hands, roll into sausage shapes. Thread 3 sosaties on to each soaked skewer.
3 Heat a thin film of oil on a pan grill or in a frying pan and, when hot, add the burgers and cook for 4–5 minutes until cooked.
4 Run a knife along one side of the baby baguettes but do not cut right through. Open them, taking care not to split them.
5 Place the peanut curry chiffonade in the base of each baguette, top with sliced tomatoes then place a sosatie burger skewer on top and close the baguette.
6 Serve with the apricot and red onion chutney on the side. Some chunky fries also go well with this burger.

Peanut curry chiffonade
40ml good quality mayonnaise
1 tbsp smooth peanut butter
1 tsp balsamic vinegar
½ tsp soy sauce
1cm piece root ginger, finely grated
pinch of cumin
pinch of sugar
salt and freshly ground black pepper
¼ iceberg lettuce, cut into chiffonade (thin shreds)
• Mix all the ingredients except the lettuce together in a bowl, seasoning to taste; add the lettuce and bind together. Chill.

Apricot and red onion chutney
75g dried apricots, thinly sliced
1 Granny Smith apple, cored and chopped
50g soaked raisins
2 red onions, thinly sliced
50g brown sugar
120ml red wine
2 tbsp corn or maple syrup
1 tbsp balsamic vinegar
• Place all the ingredients in a pan, add 200ml of water and bring to the boil.
• Reduce the heat to a simmer, cover and cook gently for 20–30 minutes.
• Uncover and continue to cook for a further 30 minutes until the onions are tender and no liquid remains. Allow to cool; store in an airtight jar ready for use.

TO SERVE • 4 BABY BAGUETTES • PEANUT CURRY CHIFFONADE • 4 TOMATOES, THINLY SLICED • APRICOT AND RED ONION CHUTNEY

Lebanese kibbeh burger with smoked chilli and white bean humous

In the Middle Eastern countries making kibbeh is an art form that requires practice to achieve perfection. I love the smoked chilli-style humous that accompanies the dish – it really adds a great kick.

150g bulghur wheat
1 onion, finely grated
1 garlic clove, crushed
1 tsp ground allspice
½ tsp ground cumin
½ tsp ground coriander
¼ tsp sweet paprika
3 tbsp chopped fresh flat-leaf parsley
650g well trimmed, coarsely minced lamb
salt and freshly ground black pepper
vegetable or sunflower oil for cooking

1 Place the bulghur wheat in a bowl, pour over enough boiling water to cover; leave to soak for 30 minutes, then drain off any remaining water left in the bowl. Dry the bulghur wheat in a towel.

2 Place the bulghur wheat in a large bowl, add the onion, garlic, spices and parsley, and allow to stand for 15 minutes.

3 Add the lamb and mix together, but do not overwork the mix. Adjust the seasoning.

4 Divide the mix into 8 evenly sized patties, then roll in the palm of your wet hands into classic torpedo oval shapes; brush with oil.

5 Heat a chargrill or pan grill until hot, add the burgers and cook for 5–6 minutes or longer if preferred.

6 Open the pitta breads, without tearing them, to form pockets; fill with the tomato, pomegranate and parsely salad, tuck in the burgers and serve with a dish of smoked chilli and white bean humous alongside.

Tomato, pomegranate and parsley salad

1 tbsp sugar
1 tsp red wine vinegar
40ml honey
1 garlic clove, crushed
75g sunblush tomatoes in 3 tbsp of their own oil
1 fresh pomegranate, halved
½ large bunch fresh flat-leaf parsley, picked and washed
50g pine nuts, toasted
salt and freshly ground black pepper

• In a pan heat the sugar and vinegar with the honey until dissolved.
• Add the garlic, tomatoes along with the oil, and cook for 1 minute. Remove to a bowl and cool.
• Squeeze out the seeds from the pomegranate halves.
• Add the parsley, pomegranate seeds and pine nuts and season.

Smoked chilli and white bean humous

15g chipotle chillies
200g cooked cannellini beans (canned is fine)
2 tbsp tahini (sesame seed) paste
½ tsp ground cumin
3 tbsp olive oil
2 small garlic cloves, crushed
juice of ½ lemon
½ tsp salt

• Reconstitute the chipotle chillies in hot water for 30 minutes, drain and discard the water. Finely chop the chillies.
• Place the beans in a blender with the chillies and remaining ingredients, and whiz to a smooth paste.
• According to taste add a little more garlic or lemon juice.
• Refrigerate overnight to infuse the flavours, covered with clingfilm.

TO SERVE • 8 MINI PITTA BREADS OR 4 PITTA BREADS, HALVED • SMOKED CHILLI AND WHITE BEAN HUMOUS • TOMATO, POMEGRANATE AND PARSLEY SALAD

Lamb burger briks with smoked aubergine hash and green harissa mayo

There is something mystical about Morocco – and its food is like its people: heartwarming. The flavours are delicate, yet simple. These Moroccan style burgers are encased in a crisp pastry shell; the aubergine hash adds a warm smoky addition to the dish.

TO SERVE · FEW SALAD LEAVES TO GARNISH · GREEN HARISSA MAYO (SEE PAGE 126)

Smoked aubergine hash

1 aubergine
90ml olive oil
1 small onion, finely chopped
1 garlic clove, crushed
1 anchovy fillet, rinsed, finely
  chopped
1 tsp smoked paprika
2 tbsp freshly chopped coriander
salt and freshly ground black
  pepper

· Preheat oven to 200°C/Gas 6.
· Brush the aubergine all over with 30ml of the olive oil.
· Place in the oven on a baking tray, bake for 30–35 minutes, turning it until it is soft and fairly charred in colour. Remove and cool.
· Cut the aubergine in half lengthways, scoop out the flesh and chop finely. Discard the skin.
· Heat the remaining oil in a frying pan, add the onion, garlic, anchovy and paprika and cook for 4–5 minutes until soft.
· Add the chopped aubergine, mix well and cook for 2–3 minutes, remove and cool. Add the chopped coriander and season to taste.

1 onion, peeled, finely chopped

1 small green pepper, deseeded, finely chopped

2 tbsp chopped fresh coriander

2.5cm piece root ginger, finely chopped

pinch of turmeric

600g well trimmed, coarsely minced lamb

1 tbsp green harissa mayo (see page 126)

salt and freshly ground black pepper

1 tbsp olive oil

8 sheets spring roll pastry

Smoked aubergine hash (see left)

1 egg, beaten with 1 tbsp milk

vegetable oil for deep frying

1 Place the onion, green pepper, coriander, ginger and turmeric in a food processor and whiz to a coarse paste. Transfer to a large bowl, add the meat, harissa mayo and season to taste. Bring the mixture together lightly, do not overwork it. Chill for 1 hour.

2 Divide the mix into 4 evenly sized burgers then, with your thumb, press down in the centre of each burger to form an indentation.

3 Heat a film of olive oil in a large nonstick frying pan; when hot, add the burgers, cook for 2–3 minutes on each side, keeping them rare. Remove from the pan and cool.

4 Lay out 4 sheets of the spring roll pastry, place some smoked aubergine hash in the centre and top with a burger.

5 Brush the outside edges with the beaten egg wash, fold the edges up and gently over the burger to enclose. Take the remaining 4 sheets and cover each burger to create a parcel, sealing the pastry neatly on top.

6 Half fill a deep fat fryer or deep, heavy based saucepan with the oil and heat it to 180°C; carefully lower the briks into the oil and fry for 2–3 minutes until golden.

7 Remove to kitchen paper and drain well.

8 Garnish with salad leaves and serve with green harissa mayo.

Neo-classical feta burger with horiatiki salsa salad and yogurt garlic sauce

Grilling the burgers in the vine leaves not only retains flavour and moistness, but also makes an unusual presentation. These little parcels can be made in advance then wrapped and kept in the refrigerator until needed.

24 brine-preserved vine leaves
600g well trimmed, coarsely minced lamb
1 garlic clove, crushed
1 tsp ground cumin
1 tsp ground coriander
1 egg yolk
salt and freshly ground black pepper
125g feta cheese, crumbled
60ml olive oil

1 Remove the vine leaves from the jar, rinse well under very cold water, then dry in a cloth.
2 Place the meat in a bowl, add the garlic, spices, and egg yolk. Season to taste.
3 Add the feta and just bring it together, but do not let it become overworked or packed too tightly.
4 Divide the mix into 8 evenly sized burgers.
5 Lay out 3 vine leaves on a flat surface, just overlapping each other.
6 Place a burger in the centre of the leaves, then wrap it up carefully like a parcel then secure with 2 cocktail sticks; prepare the others in the same way. Brush the leaves liberally all over with the olive oil.
7 Heat a chargrill or pan grill until hot, add the vine-wrapped burgers and cook over a medium heat for 5–6 minutes, turning them regularly to ensure even cooking.
8 Serve with the horiatiki salsa salad and the yogurt garlic sauce on the side.

Yogurt garlic sauce
100ml Greek yogurt
2 garlic cloves, crushed
· Mix together in a bowl, season to taste.

Horiatiki salsa salad

2 ripe but firm tomatoes, cut into chunks
1 small red onion, peeled, cut chunks
50g cucumber, peeled, cut into 1cm dice
1 small green pepper, deseeded, cut into 1cm dice
1 small green chilli, deseeded, finely chopped
12 green olives
1 tbsp chopped fresh oregano
2 tbsp roughly chopped fresh mint leaves
60ml olive oil
· Toss all the ingredients together in a bowl; leave
for 30 minutes to marinate prior to serving.

TO SERVE · HORIATIKI SALSA SALAD · YOGURT GARLIC SAUCE

Ginger–plum relish
150g ripe sweet plums (canned are
   fine), stoned, chopped
½ garlic clove, crushed
2 tbsp finely chopped stem ginger
1 tbsp Asian sweet chilli sauce
· Mix all the ingredients in a bowl,
cover with clingfilm and leave to
infuse the flavours and marinate in
the refrigerator for 24 hours.

Barbecue pork-belly burger

with sticky herb baste, ginger–plum relish, and pea and radish salad

The addition of some belly pork to the basic mix really adds a moistness and richness to the burger. The plum relish is a must! It may be kept refrigerated for up to a week.

500g well trimmed, coarsely minced pork, chilled

275g coarsely minced rindless pork belly, chilled

2 tbsp chopped fresh coriander

50g salted peanuts

2.5cm piece root ginger, finely grated

1 stick lemongrass, outer casing removed, very finely chopped

1 shallot, finely chopped

vegetable oil for cooking

FOR THE BASTE

60ml ketchup manis (Indonesian soy sauce) or light soy sauce

60ml dry sherry

2 tbsp chopped fresh coriander

1 tbsp maple syrup

1 tsp ground aniseed

½ tsp dried chilli flakes

8 wooden skewers, soaked

1 Place both pork minces in a bowl, add the remaining burger ingredients and bring the mix together. Place all the ingredients for the baste in a bowl and mix well. Add 2 tbsp of the baste to the burger mix, mix well, taking care not to overwork. Place in the refrigerator, covered, for 1 hour.

2 Heat a chargrill or pan grill until very hot. Brush the grill with a little oil. Divide the burger mix into 4 evenly sized oblong burgers and thread 2 wooden skewers through each of them.

3 Liberally brush the baste over the burgers and place on the grill, brushing them regularly with the baste and turning them until cooked, about 4–5 minutes on each side. Their appearance should be glossy and they should be sticky in texture.

4 Arrange the pea salad on the plate and top with a burger. Garnish with fresh coriander leaves and serve with a little ginger–plum relish.

TO SERVE · PEA AND RADISH SALAD · CORIANDER LEAVES TO GARNISH · GINGER–PLUM RELISH

Pea and radish salad

75g sugar snap peas
50g mange tout
6 red radishes, thinly sliced
30g roughly chopped fresh mint leaves
1 tbsp light soy sauce
1 tbsp sugar
1 tbsp rice wine vinegar
1 tsp sesame oil
salt and freshly ground black pepper

· Blanch the peas separately in boiling water for 1 minute, then refresh in ice water. Drain, then dry well. Place in a bowl, add the radishes and chopped mint.

· Heat the soy, sugar and vinegar in a small pan for 1 minute, leave to cool. Add the sesame oil, pour over the salad, toss well together, season to taste and serve.

Bulgogi barbecue burgers baked in banana leaf parcels

The flavours of the famous Korean barbecued beef dish are wonderful. Cooking in banana leaves keeps in all the aromas and natural juices. To make the leaves supple to wrap, hold them over a flame until they soften. If banana leaves are not available, use foil pouches.

700g coarsely minced pork
3 spring onions, finely chopped
2.5cm piece root ginger, finely grated
1 garlic clove, crushed
2 tbsp light soy sauce
1 tbsp Asian sweet chilli sauce
2 tsp sesame oil
1 tsp sugar
½ tsp sesame seeds, toasted
vegetable or sunflower oil for cooking

1 Mix all the ingredients for the burgers in a bowl, chill for 1 hour.
2 Divide the mix into 4 evenly sized burgers and brush liberally with the oil.
3 Heat a film of oil in a nonstick frying pan and, when hot, add the burgers; seal on each side for 1 minute then remove.
4 Place a sealed burger in the centre of each banana leaf and spoon some of the mango–coconut cream sauce over. Carefully pull up the sides of the banana leaf to enclose the burgers and make a neat parcel. Secure tightly with cocktail sticks.
5 Heat a chargrill or pan grill until hot, add the parcels and cook for 12–15 minutes or, alternatively, place in a preheated oven for 8–10 minutes.
6 Remove the parcels from the grill and serve; let the guests open them to release the wonderful aromas.

TO SERVE · 4 SQUARES OF BANANA LEAF, ABOUT 25 X 25CM · MANGO–COCONUT CREAM SAUCE (SEE PAGE 131)

Caribbean pork burgers with barbecue jerk baste and calypso mojo

450g well trimmed, coarsely minced pork
100g good quality sausage meat
1 onion, finely chopped
1 tbsp chopped fresh oregano
3 tbsp prepared jerk baste (see below)
salt and freshly ground black pepper
vegetable or sunflower oil for brushing

FOR THE JERK BASTE

45ml olive oil
2 tbsp white wine vinegar
2 tbsp hot pepper sauce
1 tbsp tomato ketchup
1 garlic clove, crushed
1 tsp dried thyme
1 tsp ground cinnamon
1 tsp sugar
1 tsp ground coriander
½ tsp ground allspice

1 For the baste, place all the ingredients in a blender and whiz until smooth.
2 Place the meat and sausage meat in a bowl, add 45ml water, the onion, oregano and 3 tbsp of the jerk baste. Adjust the seasoning, cover with cling film and chill in the refrigerator for at least 1 hour.
3 Divide the mix into 8 evenly sized burgers and brush with oil.
4 Heat a chargrill or pan grill until hot, add the burgers and grill for 8–10 minutes until cooked through, brushing them during the process with more of the baste.
5 Toast the baps; top the bases with a slice of tomato, a few dressed leaves, then 2 burgers.
6 Spoon the calypso mojo over and top with coriander leaves to garnish.

TO SERVE · 4 SESAME BURGER BAPS · 4 SLICES BEEFSTEAK TOMATOES · GREEN SALAD LEAVES DRESSED IN FRENCH DRESSING · CALYPSO MOJO (SEE PAGE 130) · FRESH CORIANDER LEAVES

Sicilian veal burger with peppers, olives and pesto crostini

800g coarsely minced veal
1 tbsp chopped fresh oregano
2 tbsp pesto sauce
1 garlic clove, crushed
50g finely chopped black olives
1 red pepper, halved, deseeded, finely chopped
1 red onion, finely chopped
salt and freshly ground black pepper
vegetable or sunflower oil for cooking

1 Combine all the burger ingredients in a bowl, add 15ml of water, mix together well and chill for 1 hour. Season the mix to taste and divide into 4 evenly sized burgers.

2 Heat a thin film of oil in a nonstick frying pan and, when hot, add the burgers and cook for 6–8 minutes until cooked.

3 Toast the ciabatta slices then spread with the pesto sauce, top with tomato slices.

4 Top with the burger, then the shaved Parmesan cheese. Garnish with the dressed rocket leaves and serve. Serve the aioli sauce on the side.

TO SERVE · 4 SLICES CIABATTA BREAD · GREEN PESTO (SEE PAGE 126) · SLICED TOMATOES · 75G FRESHLY SHAVED PARMESAN · ROCKET LEAVES DRESSED IN BALSAMIC VINEGAR · AIOLI SAUCE (SEE PAGE 126)

Vitello tonnato burger with tuna and caper sauce

vegetable or sunflower oil for cooking
1 onion, finely chopped
1 tbsp chopped fresh rosemary
450g good quality, coarsely minced veal rump
300g minced pork
1 tsp Dijon mustard
salt and freshly ground black pepper

1 Heat 2 tbsp of the oil in a frying pan and, when hot, add the onion and rosemary and cook for 4–5 minutes until softened. Transfer to a large bowl and allow to cool.
2 Add both meats, the mustard, salt and pepper to taste and chill for 1 hour.
3 Divide the meat into 4 evenly sized burgers and brush liberally with oil.
4 Heat a thin film of oil in a large frying pan, add the burgers and cook for 6–8 minutes or until cooked to your taste.
5 Split the focaccia in half horizontally to give 4 bases. Top each with some tuna and caper sauce, then top with a burger.
6 Top each burger with 2 slices of beefsteak tomato and then with some rocket leaves, dressed in the black olive dressing. Sprinkle the toasted pine nuts over and serve.

Tuna and caper sauce
100g canned tuna in oil, well drained
1 small garlic clove, crushed
2 anchovy fillets in oil, drained, chopped
2 tsp capers, rinsed, chopped
75ml good quality mayonnaise
1 tbsp chopped fresh chives
1 tbsp fresh lemon juice
• Place the tuna, garlic, anchovies and capers in a blender, whiz to a smooth purée, remove to a bowl.
• Mix with the mayonnaise, chives, add lemon juice, seasoning to taste. Keep chilled ready for use.

Black olive dressing
40g black olives, pitted and finely chopped
75ml olive oil
juice of ½ lemon
1 tsp balsamic vinegar
2 tbsp chopped fresh chives
• Mix all the ingredients together, seasoning to taste.

TO SERVE • 2 X 10CM SQUARES FOCACCIA BREAD • TUNA AND CAPER SAUCE • 8 SLICES BEEFSTEAK TOMATOES • 50G ROCKET LEAVES, WASHED • 60ML BLACK OLIVE DRESSING • 2 TBSP TOASTED PINE NUTS

Cordon bleu burger with melting Brie and caramelised apple butter

700g well trimmed, coarsely minced
  chicken
1 onion, finely chopped
1 tbsp chopped fresh rosemary
salt and freshly ground black pepper
vegetable or sunflower oil for cooking
120g thinly sliced gammon ham
25g caster sugar
1 Granny Smith apple, peeled, cored, cut
  into small chunks
25g unsalted butter
4 x 1cm thick wedges of Brie cheese

1 Combine the chicken with 45ml water, the onion and rosemary in a bowl, season to taste;
  cover and refrigerate for 1 hour.
2 Divide into 4 evenly sized burgers and brush liberally with oil.
3 Heat a chargrill or pan grill until very hot, add the burgers and cook for 4–5 minutes each
  side or longer if you prefer, keep them warm. Grill the ham slices on each side, keep warm.
4 Meanwhile heat the sugar in a pan, add the apple pieces and cook until lightly caramelised;
  add the butter and 2 tbsp water, cover with a lid and cook to a compote; season to taste.
5 Place a wedge of Brie cheese on each burger and place under a preheated grill until the
  cheese is just melted.
6 Place some watercress in the base of each roll, followed by a slice of gammon ham. Top
  with a burger and a good spoonful of caramelised apple butter, cover with the roll lid and
  serve immediately.

TO SERVE · 4 CRUSTY ROLLS, SPLIT · 50G WATERCRESS LEAVES

Chicken steak burger with Provençal flavours

650g skinless, boneless chicken breast

salt and freshly ground black pepper

150g panko crumbs or fresh white breadcrumbs

75ml milk

2 tbsp chopped fresh basil

50g finely grated Parmigiano Reggianno cheese

flour for dusting

2 eggs, beaten

vegetable oil or sunflower oil for cooking

4 slices firm goats' cheese log

Black olive tapenade
1 anchovy fillet, rinsed, chopped
2 tbsp superfine capers
40g black olives, pitted
75ml olive oil
1 garlic cove, crushed
2 tbsp chopped fresh flat-leaf parsley
salt and freshly ground black pepper
· Place all the ingredients in a blender and whiz to a coarse paste; adjust seasoning and serve.

1 Place the chicken and a little seasoning in a food processor with 50g of the panko crumbs and whiz to a coarse pulp. Add the milk, whiz again for 20 seconds. Add the chopped basil then remove to a bowl and chill for 30 minutes.

2 Flour your hands and shape the mix into 4 evenly sized burgers.

3 Mix the remaining panko crumbs and Parmesan. Pass the burgers through extra flour, then through the beaten egg wash, then into the panko Parmesan mix; reshape if necessary.

4 Heat a thin film of oil in a nonstick frying pan, add the burgers and fry until golden.

5 Toast the baps and spoon some mayonnaise on the bases, add a few rocket leaves and some green pesto.

6 Place the chicken burger on top, then a slice of the goats' cheese. Place under a hot grill for 30 seconds to melt the cheese. Drizzle some black olive tapenade over, and close the baps and serve.

TO SERVE · 4 PLAIN BAPS, SPLIT · 60ML MAYONNAISE (SEE PAGE 126) · ROCKET SALAD DRESSED IN BALSAMIC DRESSING · GREEN PESTO · (SEE PAGE 126) · BLACK OLIVE TAPENADE

Smoked chicken cobb burger with watercress and tomato yogurt

The idea for this burger came from the classical American cobb salad that I just enjoyed in Florida. I loved the idea of chicken, avocado and blue cheese in harmony and I decided to create a smoked chicken burger around the theme.

500g well trimmed, coarsely minced
  chicken breast
250g skinless smoked chicken breasts,
  finely diced
1 small onion, finely chopped
1 tsp Dijon mustard

1 tbsp tomato ketchup
1 tsp hot pepper sauce
1 tbsp sour cream
salt and freshly ground black pepper
vegetable or sunflower oil for cooking

1 In a bowl mix together the chicken breast with the finely diced smoked chicken.
2 Add the onion, mustard, ketchup and chilli sauce, bind together; add the sour cream and seasoning and bind together for a final time. Chill for 1 hour in the refrigerator.
3 Using wet hands, divide the mix into 4 evenly sized burgers. Brush the burgers liberally with the oil.
4 Heat a chargrill or pan grill until hot, add the burgers and cook for 4–5 minutes on each side until golden.
5 Toast the muffins or baps on the grill pan until golden, top with some shredded endive. Add the burger and then some sliced avocado and thinly sliced onion.
6 Finally sprinkle the crumbled blue cheese over and pass under a hot grill to melt the cheese; serve with the watercress and tomato yogurt.

Watercress and tomato yogurt
50g watercress, stalks removed
2 plum tomatoes, peeled, deseeded, chopped
1 small red onion, finely chopped
100ml sour cream
75g sweetcorn kernels, drained
salt and freshly ground black pepper
• Mix all the ingredients together in a bowl, season to taste.

TO SERVE · 4 ENGLISH MUFFINS OR BURGER BAPS, SPLIT · 1 BELGIAN RED ENDIVE, LEAVES SEPARATED, SHREDDED · 1 SMALL RED ONION, PEELED, THINLY SLICED · 1 AVOCADO, PEELED, THINLY SLICED · 100G GORGONZOLA CHEESE, CRUMBLED · WATERCRESS AND TOMATO YOGURT

Barbecue chicken burger

with Thai spices, green chilli relish and coconut–lemongrass chutney

The ingredients in this Asian burger are typical of Thai cooking, giving it a sensual flavour and aroma, and they are all now easily accessible for the cook. When preparing the chilli relish use a mild variety.

1 tbsp red curry paste (rempah)

2 sticks lemongrass, tough outer casing removed, very finely chopped

¼ tsp turmeric

2.5cm piece root ginger, peeled, finely grated

500g minced chicken breasts, well chilled

250g minced pork, well chilled

3 kaffir lime leaves, finely chopped

2 tbsp chopped fresh Thai basil (holy basil)

1 tbsp chopped fresh coriander

2 tbsp coconut milk

pinch each ground cumin and ground coriander

salt and freshly ground black pepper

vegetable oil for cooking

1 In a bowl mix together the curry paste, lemongrass, turmeric and ginger. Add the minced meats and mix well with wet hands to bring all the ingredients together.

2 Add the lime leaves, fresh herbs, coconut milk, ground spices and seasoning. Bring together again, but do not overwork. Place in the refrigerator to chill.

3 With wet hands, shape into 4 evenly sized burgers. Heat a pan grill.

4 Brush the burgers with a little oil, place on the grill, and cook for 6–8 minutes until golden and cooked, turning them regularly.

5 Toast the burger baps, spread the bottom baps liberally with the green chilli relish and top each with a slice of beef tomato.

6 Place the burgers on top and garnish with the coconut–lemongrass chutney; close with the lid and serve.

Green chilli relish

100ml rice wine vinegar

60g soft brown sugar

75g raisins, soaked in water for 15 minutes, then drained

2 shallots, finely chopped

2 green peppers, deseeded, chopped

150g mild green chillis, deseeded, finely chopped (Dutch lombok variety)

½ tbsp chopped root ginger

1 garlic clove, crushed

1 tsp nam pla (fish sauce)

• Place the vinegar and sugar in a small pan and bring to the boil. Add the raisins and cook to a light caramel, the liquid should be syrupy.

• Stir in the shallots, green pepper, chillies, ginger and garlic. Cook for 3-4 minutes, add the fish sauce, then remove from the heat and leave to cool.

• Place in a blender, whiz to a coarse purée, serve chilled.

Coconut–lemongrass chutney

250g red cherry tomatoes

3 tbsp honey

juice of 3 limes

1 fresh coconut, outer shell removed, coarsely grated

2 tbsp unsalted peanuts

1 small green chilli, deseeded, finely chopped

1 tbsp chopped pickled pink ginger

2 sticks lemongrass, outer casing removed, finely chopped

2 tbsp coarsely chopped fresh coriander

1 tbsp coarsely chopped fresh mint

• Cut the cherry tomatoes in half, and place in a bowl, add the honey and lime juice, leave for 30 minutes to release their juices.

• Add the remaining ingredients, toss well together, leave to marinate for a further 2 hours before use.

TO SERVE · 4 BURGER BAPS, SPLIT · 4 SLICES BEEF TOMATOES · GREEN CHILLI RELISH · COCONUT–LEMONGRASS CHUTNEY

Bengali chicken burger with cucumber and tomato achar and Asian guacamole

Bengal lies in the north east of India; it is famed for its art and wonderful food festivals which are an everyday part of Bengali life. The popular blend of spices used in this burger is more commonly known as 'panch phoran': a five-spice mixture with a unique flavour.

¼ tsp fennel seeds
¼ tsp cumin seeds
¼ tsp nigella seeds (kalongi)
⅛ tsp black mustard seeds
⅛ tsp fenugreek
650g coarsely minced, skinless, boneless chicken breast
150g good quality sausage meat
salt and freshly ground black pepper
vegetable or sunflower oil for cooking

1 Heat a dry nonstick frying pan and, when hot, add the fennel seeds, cumin, nigella seeds, mustard seeds and fenugreek and toss for 30 seconds so that they give off their aroma and fragrance.
2 Place in a mortar and pestle and crush to a fine powder.
3 Place both meats in a bowl, add the crushed spices and season to taste. Chill for 1 hour.
4 Divide the mix into 4 evenly sized burgers and brush liberally with oil.
5 Heat a chargrill or pan grill until hot, add the burgers and cook for 6–8 minutes until golden.
6 Toast the baps; place some Asian guacamole on the base of each and top each with a cooked burger. Spoon the cucumber and tomato achar over, close the lid and serve. Serve the sour cream alongside.

TO SERVE • 4 SESAME SEED BURGER BAPS, SPLIT (SEE PAGE 135) • ASIAN GUACAMOLE (SEE PAGE 130) • CUCUMBER AND TOMATO ACHAR • 60ML SOUR CREAM

Cucumber and tomato achar

15ml vegetable oil
1 onion, chopped
1 garlic clove, crushed
1 tsp curry paste
4 tomatoes, skinned, deseeded, diced
¼ cucumber, peeled, cut into 0.5cm dice
salt
lime juice to taste
2 tbsp chopped fresh coriander

• Heat the oil in a small pan, add the onion and garlic and cook for 3–4 minutes until tender. Add the curry paste and cook for a further 2 minutes.
• Add the tomatoes and cucumber; cook for 2–3 minutes until they begin to soften. Season to taste.
• Remove to a bowl, allow to go cold. Add the lime juice to give it a sour note, stir in the coriander and serve.

Chermoula burgers with minted harissa salsa and preserved lemon and artichoke salad

Chermoula is a fragrant, aromatic Moroccan spice paste, used as a sauce or as a marinade base for flavouring fish, meats and vegetables. In this recipe the ground spices permeate the meats lending an exotic flavour to a simple preparation.

650g coarsely minced skinless, boneless chicken breast

100g merguez sausage, cut into 0.5cm dice

1 onion, peeled, finely chopped

1 garlic clove, crushed

1 small green chilli, deseeded, finely chopped

1 tsp cumin seeds, toasted, crushed

1 tbsp coriander seeds, toasted, crushed

¼ tsp paprika

¼ tsp turmeric

salt and freshly ground black pepper

vegetable or sunflower oil for cooking

4 wooden skewers, soaked

1 Mix all the ingredients for the burgers in a bowl with 30ml of water. Season the mixture to taste and chill for 1 hour.

2 Divide the mix into 8 evenly sized burgers, then, with wet hands, shape each burger around a wooden skewer in a sausage shape; brush liberally with oil.

3 Heat a chargrill or pan grill until hot, place the skewers on it and chargrill for 6–8 minutes, turning them regularly and keeping the exposed part of the wooden skewer away from the heat to avoid burning.

4 Open the flatbreads, remove the burgers from the skewers and place inside then spoon some harissa salsa over. Serve with the preserved lemon and artichoke salad.

TO SERVE • 4 WARM MIDDLE EASTERN FLATBREADS OR PITTAS • MINTED HARISSA SALSA • PRESERVED LEMON AND ARTICHOKE SALAD

Preserved lemon and artichoke salad

150g preserved artichokes in oil,
   drained (oil reserved), cut in half
1 garlic clove, crushed
2 tbsp flaked almonds, toasted
1 tbsp preserved lemon, finely
   diced
45ml honey
juice of 1 lemon
2 tbsp chopped fresh coriander

• Heat 2 tbsp of the artichoke oil in
a pan, add the garlic, and cook for
20 seconds. Add the almonds,
preserved lemon and honey and
cook for 2 minutes longer. Add the
lemon juice, mix well.
• Pour into a bowl, add the
artichokes, mix well to meld the
flavours and leave to go cold.
• Sprinkle the coriander over
and serve.

Minted harissa salsa

4 plum tomatoes, skinned,
   deseeded, chopped
2 spring onions, chopped
1 red onion, chopped
2 tbsp chopped fresh mint
1 tbsp maple syrup
½ garlic cove, crushed
juice of ½ lemon
½ tsp good quality harissa sauce

• Mix all the ingredients together;
for the best flavour, leave to infuse
overnight in the refrigerator.

Bacon-wrapped turkey burger

with melted Camembert, and spicy cranberry–green peppercorn relish

800g coarsely minced skinless turkey breast, chilled

1 tsp Dijon mustard

2 tbsp chopped fresh flat-leaf parsley

15g unsalted butter

2 spring onions, finely chopped

2 tsp picked fresh thyme leaves

1 small garlic clove, crushed

salt and freshly ground black pepper

vegetable or sunflower oil for cooking

8 rashers streaky bacon

olive oil

¼ Camembert cheese

1 In a bowl mix together the turkey mince, 15ml of water, the mustard and parsley.

2 Heat the butter in a small frying pan and, when hot, add the spring onions, half the thyme, the garlic and cook for 1 minute. Allow to cool, then add to the mince mixture; season to taste. Chill in the refrigerator for up to 1 hour.

3 Form the mix into 4 evenly sized burgers. Wrap each burger in 2 rashers of bacon, then secure each with a cocktail stick. Brush the burgers with a little olive oil.

4 Heat a chargrill or pan grill until very hot. Place the burgers on the grill and cook for 5 minutes on each side or until cooked through.

5 Using a cookie cutter, cut out a 7.5–8cm circle out of each slice of brioche and toast under a preheated grill. Place some watercress on each of the brioche slices, then top with the burger.

6 Cut the Camembert into 1cm thick slices and place one on each burger. Sprinkle the remaining thyme over, drizzle with a little olive oil and place under the grill again until the cheese begins to melt. Top with a good dollop of the relish, garnish with a thyme sprig and serve.

TO SERVE • 4 X SLICES OF BRIOCHE LOAF (SEE PAGE 136) • 50G WATERCRESS • SPICY CRANBERRY–GREEN PEPPERCORN RELISH (SEE PAGE 131) • FRESH THYME SPRIGS TO GARNISH

Turkey BLT burger stack

600g minced skinless turkey
  breast
1 tsp Dijon mustard
1 tsp chopped fresh oregano
1 tsp Worcestershire sauce
1 tsp tomato ketchup
salt and freshly ground black
  pepper
vegetable or sunflower oil for
  cooking
4 long wooden skewers

FOR THE LETTUCE MAYONNAISE
60ml good quality mayonnaise
75g shredded iceberg lettuce
1 small onion, finely chopped
½ tsp American-style mustard
50g dill pickles, finely chopped

1 Mix all the hamburger ingredients in a bowl
  with 15ml water, chill for 1 hour.
2 Divide the mix into 8 evenly sized burgers,
  brush liberally with the oil.
3 Heat a chargrill or pan grill until very hot.
  Place the burgers on the grill and cook for
  4–5 minutes or longer if preferred. Grill the
  smoked bacon.
4 Mix all the ingredients together for the
  lettuce mayonnaise, season to taste.
5 Cut the baps into 3 horizontal slices and
  toast the bap slices. Place a good
  spoonful of cooked tomato relish on
  the base baps.
6 Top each with a burger, then some
  lettuce mayonnaise, and grilled
  smoked bacon. Add a toasted
  slice of bap and another
  spoonful of tomato relish.
7 Finally add some tomato
  slices, grilled bacon, a second
  burger, and more lettuce
  mayonnaise. Close with the bap
  lid and plunge a wooden skewer
  into the centre to keep it in place.

TO SERVE • 4 SESAME BURGER BAPS • 8 SLICES SMOKED STREAKY BACON
• COOKED TOMATO RELISH (SEE PAGE 129) • 4 TOMATOES, THINLY SLICED

Peking duck wraps with hoisin barbecue sauce

These delicate little pastry-wrapped triangles are filled with a Chinese-style patty; cooked Peking duck can be found in most supermarkets now. These wraps can be frozen then cooked when needed, although they will take an extra 10 minutes cooking.

2 x 150g skinless, boneless chicken breasts
350g cooked Peking duck, meat and skin only
30ml vegetable oil
2 tbsp oyster sauce
2 tbsp chopped fresh coriander
1 small garlic clove, crushed
1 tsp Chinese five spices
1 tsp barbecue hoisin sauce
½ small red chilli, deseeded, finely chopped
salt and freshly ground black pepper
8 sheets filo pastry (30 x 18cm)
50g butter, melted, for brushing

Hoisin barbecue sauce

1 tbsp dark brown sugar
2 tbsp tomato ketchup
1 garlic clove, crushed
2.5cm piece root ginger
1 tsp rice wine vinegar
90ml hoisin sauce
30ml Asian sweet chilli sauce
1 star anis pod
½ tbsp finely chopped lemongrass

• In a pan, combine the sugar, ketchup, garlic and ginger with the vinegar; bring to the boil. Add the hoisin, sweet chilli sauce, the star anise, lemongrass and 150ml water. Simmer for 15–20 minutes, until reduced by one third in volume. Remove the star anise and transfer the sauce to a bowl; allow to go cold before serving.

TO SERVE · FRESH CORIANDER LEAVES TO GARNISH · HOISIN BARBECUE SAUCE

1 Preheat oven to 200°C/Gas 6. Place the chicken meat and cooked duck in a food processor and whiz to a coarse paste. Add the remaining filling ingredients and whiz again quickly until incorporated; season to taste. Using wet hands, shape the mix into 8 evenly sized balls.
2 Fold one sheet of filo in half lengthways, then fold over the corner at one end of the the pastry strip, over one meatball, covering it in a triangle shape. (Wonton wraps or spring roll pastry can also be used.)
3 Continue folding over the triangle of pastry along the length of the filo pastry strip to make a neat triangular samosa shape. Make 3 more samosa shapes in the same way.
4 Place them on a baking sheet, brush liberally with melted butter all over, and bake for 12–15 minutes or until golden. Garnish with fresh coriander leaves and serve with the hoisin barbecue sauce separately.

Pheasant burger with foie gras, honey mustard glaze and spicy kumquat chutney

Every year I eagerly look forward to the game season – and a real gourmet treat. The addition of a little pork and foie gras to these burgers adds flavour and also keeps them moist and juicy. The spicy cranberry–green peppercorn relish on page 131 would go well.

400g coarsely minced skinless, boneless
　pheasant breast
300g coarsely minced pork
100g fresh foie gras, deveined, cut into
　0.5cm cubes
1 shallot, finely chopped
4 juniper berries, finely chopped
2 tsp chopped fresh sage
salt and freshly ground black pepper
vegetable or sunflower oil for cooking

FOR THE GLAZE
1 tsp Dijon mustard
75ml honey
15ml olive oil
½ tsp soy sauce

1 In a bowl combine the pheasant, pork and foie gras. Add the shallot, juniper and sage along with a little salt and pepper, chill for 1 hour.
2 Divide the mix into 4 evenly sized burgers.
3 Heat a chargrill or pan grill until very hot, and brush the burgers liberally with oil.
4 Combine the ingredients for the glaze in a bowl.
5 Place the burgers on the grill and cook for 5–8 minutes, brushing them regularly with the glaze as they cook.
6 Toast the baps, and top the 4 bases with some spicy kumquat chutney, then with some rocket leaves, followed by the glazed pheasant burger and serve.

Spicy kumquat chutney
200g sugar
350ml white wine vinegar
500g kumquats, halved
1 jalepeño chilli, deseeded, finely
　chopped
2.5cm piece root ginger, finely
　grated
• Place the sugar and vinegar in a pan and bring to the boil, stirring, to dissolve the sugar. When boiled raise the heat and add the kumquats, chilli and ginger. Simmer gently for 30 minutes until the mix becomes thick and jam-like in consistency.
• Cool before use, serve warm or cold.

TO SERVE · 2 CHORIZO BURGER BAPS, SPLIT (SEE PAGE 135) · SPICY KUMQUAT CHUTNEY · 50G ROCKET LEAVES

Ostrich burger with cumin seed and guava ketchup, and tempura sweet potatoes

1 tsp cumin seeds
450g cleaned ostrich fillet, coarsely
  minced
250g minced pork
15ml olive oil
1 garlic clove, crushed
½ tsp freshly grated orange zest
½ tsp ground cinnamon
salt and freshly ground black pepper
vegetable or sunflower oil for cooking

1 Heat a dry frying pan over a medium heat, add the cumin seeds and dry fry for 10–15 seconds, keeping them moving so they do not burn. Transfer to a mortar and pestle and crush to a fine powder.

2 Place both meats in a bowl with 45ml water; add the cumin seeds, olive oil, garlic, orange zest and cinnamon. Mix well together but do not overwork; season to taste. Chill for 1 hour.

3 Divide the mix into 4 evenly sized burgers and brush liberally with oil.

4 Heat a chargrill or pan grill until very hot, add the burgers and cook for 4–5 minutes on each side until cooked.

5 Toast the burger baps, spread a thin layer of mustard on the bases. Place some shredded iceberg lettuce on each base.

6 Top each base with a burger, then pour over a little cumin seed and guava ketchup and top with a lid. Serve with tempura sweet potatoes on the side.

Cumin seed and guava ketchup
100ml guava jam
2 tbsp tomato ketchup
1 tbsp treacle or molasses
30ml red wine vinegar
1 tsp Dijon mustard
1 tsp ground cumin seeds
1 garlic clove
¼ tsp ground cinnamon
pinch of ground cloves
• Combine all the ingredients in a pan. Bring to the boil, reduce the heat and cook for 15 minutes. Remove from the heat; allow to go cold before use.

TO SERVE • 4 BURGER BAPS, SPLIT • DIJON MUSTARD • SHREDDED ICEBERG LETTUCE
• CUMIN SEED AND GUAVA KETCHUP • TEMPURA SWEET POTATOES (SEE PAGE 140)

Green papaya ponzu sauce

juice of 1 lime
60ml olive oil
1 tsp rice wine vinegar
1 green papaya, peeled, finely sliced
½ small red chilli, deseeded, finely shredded
3 spring onions, finely shredded lengthways
1 roasted red pepper, deseeded, finely shredded
2 tbsp chopped fresh coriander

• Combine the lime juice, olive oil and vinegar in a bowl. Add the fruit and vegetables, toss gently together. Add the coriander and leave for 30 minutes to infuse the flavours.

TO SERVE
• 4 SESAME BURGER BAPS, SPLIT
• 75G THINLY SLICED CUCUMBER
• WASABI MAYO (SEE PAGE 126)
• GREEN PAPAYA PONZU SAUCE
• CORIANDER LEAVES TO GARNISH
• SHISO CRESS TO GARNISH

5-spice rubbed quail burger with green papaya ponzu sauce, and wasabi mayo

600g well trimmed, coarsely minced, skinless, boneless quails
200g minced turkey breast
4 spring onions, finely chopped
1 red chilli, deseeded, finely chopped
1 garlic clove, crushed
2.5cm piece root ginger, finely grated
1 tbsp light soy sauce
1 tsp Chinese five-spice mixture
salt and freshly ground black pepper
vegetable or sunflower oil for cooking

1 Place the quail and turkey breast meat in a bowl with 45ml water, add the spring onions, red chilli, garlic clove, ginger, soy sauce, half the five-spice mixture, and salt and pepper and mix well. Cover with clingfilm and chill for 1 hour.

2 Divide the mix into 4 evenly sized burgers, brush liberally with oil all over, then season with the remaining five-spice mixture.

3 Heat a chargrill or pan grill until hot, add the burgers and cook for 4–5 minutes until cooked, or a little longer if you prefer.

4 Toast the baps; cover the bases with sliced cucumber.

5 Top with a good dollop of wasabi mayo, followed by the burgers.

6 Top with the green papaya ponzu sauce, coriander leaves and shiso cress. Replace the lids and serve.

Venison burger with grilled pineapple and chilli mayo

Andrew Blake is a talented restaurateur from Australia, and this recipe is from his magnificent book published some years ago called *Blakes* – and demonstrates a wonderful yet simple combination of ingredients.

1 small onion, minced
2 garlic cloves, minced
olive oil for cooking
600g minced venison
200g pork fat, minced
1 tbsp chopped fresh sage
2 eggs
salt and freshly ground black
  pepper
4 rings of fresh pineapple
8 thin slices Gruyère cheese

1 Sweat the onion and garlic in a little olive oil for 2 minutes on a medium heat. Cool and place in a mixing bowl with the minced venison and pork fat, sage and eggs; mix well and season.
2 Form into 4 large patties, about 2–3cm thick.
3 In a heavy based frying pan, cook the venison patties in a little olive oil to a medium-rare stage.
4 Preheat the grill and grill the pineapple, and in the last 30 seconds or so, place 2 slices of Gruyère cheese on each ring to melt.
5 Cut the burger baps in half and toast the 4 halves on both sides.
6 On each bap half, place a small amount of rocket, followed by slices of tomato, a venison burger, a cheesy pineapple ring, and finally onion rings. Drizzle the chilli mayo over and serve.

TO SERVE · 2 BURGER BAPS · 50G ROCKET SALAD LEAVES · 2 VINE RIPENED TOMATOES, SLICED · CRISPY FRIED ONION RINGS · 100ML CHILLI MAYO (SEE PAGE 126)

Crispy fried onion rings
250g plain flour
60g cornflour
300ml sparkling beer
300ml soda water
2 Spanish onions, sliced into
  rings
vegetable or sunflower oil for
  deep frying

· Place the flours in a large bowl and whisk together; add the beer and soda water, and mix well to incorporate. Whisk vigorously to get rid of any lumps.
· Let it stand for 10 minutes, then whisk again for 30 seconds.
· Half fill a deep fat fryer or deep, heavy based saucepan with the oil and heat it to 180°C.
· Dip the onion rings in the batter and fry for 2–3 minutes until golden. Drain on kitchen paper.

Pesto salmon burger with balsamic grilled asparagus

Pesto salmon burger with balsamic grilled asparagus

600g fresh skinless, boneless salmon fillet,
  cut into large chunks
2 tbsp pesto (home-made or shop bought)
1 egg white
50g fresh white breadcrumbs
1 shallot, peeled, finely chopped
salt and freshly ground black pepper
olive oil for cooking

Balsamic grilled asparagus
12 asparagus spears, peeled,
  woody base stem removed
30ml olive oil
10ml balsamic vinegar
¼ tsp Dijon mustard
• Blanch the asparagus spears in boiling
salted water for 2 minutes, then remove with
a slotted spoon. Dry on kitchen towel.
• Heat a chargrill or pan grill until hot. In a
bowl combine the oil, vinegar and mustard
to form a baste.
• Pass the asparagus spears through the
baste mixture and place on the hot grill to
cook until golden and lightly charred, basting
regularly, about 3–4 minutes in total.

1 Place the salmon, pesto, egg white, breadcrumbs, shallot, and salt and pepper in a food processor and whiz until the salmon is finely chopped, but not puréed. Chill in the refrigerator for 30 minutes.
2 Divide the mixture into 8 evenly sized salmon burgers.
3 Heat a little olive oil in a large nonstick frying pan over medium heat. Add the burgers and cook for 2–3 minutes on each side until golden; do not overcook.
4 Cut the focaccia in half horizontally and toast them, then brush the cut sides with the oil.
5 To serve, arrange 3 asparagus on each toasted focaccia. Top each with 2 salmon burgers.
6 Place a good dollop of marscapone on top, followed by a drizzle of pesto sauce and garnish with the basil leaves.

TO SERVE · 2 X 10CM SQUARES FOCACCIA BREAD · BALSAMIC GRILLED ASPARAGUS
· 75ML MARSCAPONE CHEESE · 60ML GREEN PESTO (SEE PAGE 126)
· FRESH BASIL LEAVES TO GARNISH

Fajita salmon burger

500g fresh skinless, boneless salmon fillet,
  well chilled
salt and freshly ground black pepper
½ tsp paprika
1 egg white
100g fresh white breadcrumbs
vegetable or sunflower oil for cooking
1 onion, thinly sliced
1 garlic clove, crushed
½ tsp chopped fresh oregano
1 small red pepper, roasted, shredded
pinch of chilli powder
100g Monterey Jack or Cheddar cheese,
  grated

1 Place the salmon fillet in a food processor with a little salt, paprika and the egg white, and whiz to a smooth purée. Add the breadcrumbs, whiz again, season to tase and remove to a bowl. Chill for 1 hour.
2 Divide the mix into 4 evenly sized balls, then roll out using wet hands to sausage shapes about 2.5cm thick.
3 Heat a thin film of oil in a frying pan and, when hot, add the burgers and cook for 4–5 minutes until cooked; keep the burgers warm.
4 Return the pan to the heat, add a little more oil, the onion and garlic, and cook for 2–3 minutes. Add the oregano, shredded red pepper, chilli powder and cook for 1 minute. Stir in the cheese and immediately remove from the heat.
5 Using a dry frying pan, heat it until hot, add the tortillas one at a time and lightly char on each side; keep them warm.
6 Place one cooked burger in each tortilla, spoon the red pepper mix over and roll up to secure. Cut each in half on a diagonal. Arrange 2 halves on each serving plate, spoon the tomato salsa over, and top with a good dollop of sour cream; garnish with lime wedges and coriander leaves.

TO SERVE · 4 FLOUR TORTILLAS · FRESH TOMATO SALSA (SEE PAGE 131) · 100ML SOUR CREAM · LIME WEDGES · FRESH CORIANDER LEAVES TO GARNISH

Fajita salmon burger

Miso-basted salmon burger with hot mango–cucumber salsa and cool chilli verde

Miso is a Japanese condiment made from bean paste that embodies the essence of Japanese cooking. There are different types of miso – in this recipe the rich flavour of salmon is delicately combined with a sweet and savoury glaze made using white miso.

600g fresh skinless, boneless salmon fillet

1 tsp white miso paste

2 tbsp vegetable oil

1 shallot, finely chopped

2.5cm piece root ginger, peeled, finely chopped

salt

75g fresh white breadcrumbs

2 spring onions, finely chopped

1 large egg white

1 tbsp light soy sauce

1 tsp sesame oil

½ tsp mustard seeds

FOR THE GLAZE

½ tbsp white miso paste

2 tbsp maple syrup

1 tsp soy sauce

1 In a small bowl, mix together the ingredients for the glaze and set aside.

2 Place 350g of the salmon in a food processor with 1 tsp of the miso and whiz to a fine paste. Finely chop the remaining salmon. Chill separately in the refrigerator for 20 minutes.

3 Heat 1 tbsp of the vegetable oil in a small pan, add the shallot and ginger and cook until softened but with no colour; remove and allow to cool.

4 Remove the processed and chopped salmon from the refrigerator, place in a bowl; add the cooked shallot and ginger, a little salt and mix well.

5 Add the remaining ingredients and bring the mix together, shape into 4 evenly sized burgers and return to the refrigerator until needed.

6 Heat the remaining oil in a large nonstick frying pan until hot, cook the salmon burgers until golden, about 3–4 minutes on each side, brushing them regularly with the glaze as they cook.

7 Arrange the lettuce leaves on the 4 crusty rolls, top each with a burger, and then with some mango–cucumber salsa. Top with the remaining bread. Serve with a little pot of cool chilli verde on the side.

Hot mango–cucumber salsa

1 small mango, stone removed, cut in thin slices

¼ cucumber, cut in ribbons lengthways, using a vegetable peeler

1 tsp sugar

2 tbsp lime juice

salt

good pinch of dried chilli flakes

• Place all the ingredients together in a bowl, toss well together, leave until required.

Cool chilli verde

3 green peppers, deseeded

1 green chilli, deseeded

2 tbsp chopped fresh coriander

2 spring onions, finely chopped

1 tbsp crème fraîche

2 tbsp rice wine vinegar

1 tbsp sugar

¼ tsp Chinese mustard

• Place the peppers, chilli, coriander and spring onions in a small blender, whiz to a coarse purée, remove to a bowl.

• Add the remaining ingredients, whiz again, and leave to infuse for 1 hour or preferably overnight.

TO SERVE · 4 CRUSTY ROLLS OR BAPS, SPLIT · 8 GREEN BUTTER LETTUCE LEAVES
· HOT MANGO–CUCUMBER SALSA · COOL CHILLI VERDE

Smoked-salmon burger bagel

with egg and caper relish, and quark and sweet mustard cream

Smoked salmon set on a lightly toasted bagel, topped with cream cheese, tiny sliced shallots and capers is a classic Jewish speciality. Taking this theme I have created an alternative made from potato and smoked fish. Easy to prepare and extremely healthy!

2 large potatoes, peeled
1 small onion, finely chopped
250g skinless, boneless white fish
   fillet (e.g. haddock, cod, halibut)
250g smoked salmon, coarsely
   chopped
salt and freshly ground black pepper
oil for cooking
flour for dusting

1 Using a grater, coarsely grate the potatoes and place in a cloth, then squeeze out the excess water. Place in a bowl, and add the onion.
2 Place the white fish and smoked salmon in a food processor with a little freshly ground black pepper. Whiz quickly to a smooth paste, then remove and add to the potatoes and onion. Adjust the seasoning.
3 Shape into 4 evenly sized burgers.
4 Heat a nonstick frying pan and, when hot, add the oil to a depth of 1cm. Dust the burgers lightly with flour, and fry them for 2–3 minutes each side, then remove and drain them on kitchen paper.
5 Toast the bagels and spread liberally with the quark and sweet mustard cream. Place some smoked salmon over, some baby spinach leaves, and top with the smoked salmon burger.
6 Spoon some egg and caper relish over, top with thinly sliced shallot rings and serve.

TO SERVE • 4 FRESH BAGELS, SPLIT • 80G SLICED SMOKED SALMON • BABY SPINACH LEAVES • 2 LARGE SHALLOTS, PEELED AND THINLY SLICED • QUARK AND SWEET MUSTARD CREAM • EGG AND CAPER RELISH

Quark and sweet mustard cream

1 tsp sweet mustard
1 small garlic clove, crushed
salt and freshly ground black
  pepper
100ml quark cheese or other soft
  cheese
2 tbsp chopped fresh dill
• Place the mustard, garlic and a little seasoning in a bowl, mix well
• Beat in the quark until smooth and creamy.
• Add the dill, mix well, adjust the seasoning.

Egg and caper relish

½ tsp Dijon mustard
3 hard boiled eggs, coarsely
  chopped
1 shallot, finely chopped
10g cocktail capers, coarsely
  chopped
1 tbsp chopped fresh flat-leaf
  parsley
60ml good quality French
  dressing
• Mix all together, leave to infuse for 30 minutes.

Tuna burger with cabbage tzatziki

Marcus Samuelsson originates from Sweden but lives in New York where he is chef at the Aquavit: one of the city's hottest restaurants – this recipe comes from his book *Aquavit: and the new Scandinavian cuisine*.

250g tuna steak, cut into 0.5cm dice
6 large sea scallops, cleaned, cut into 0.5cm dice
1 tbsp pickled ginger, finely chopped
2 garlic cloves, finely chopped
1 tbsp chopped fresh coriander
1 tbsp Asian sweet chilli sauce
1 tsp wasabi powder
50ml freshly squeezed lime juice
sea salt and freshly ground black pepper
olive oil for cooking

1 In a medium bowl, combine the tuna, scallops, ginger, garlic, coriander, chilli sauce, wasabi and lime juice, mixing well; season with salt and pepper. Let stand for 10 minutes, then transfer to a strainer, set over a bowl, to drain off any excess liquid.

2 Split the focaccia in half and toast lightly, brush the cut sides with a little of the olive oil.

3 Shape the tuna mixture into 4 patties. Heat some olive oil in a large skillet over a medium high heat until hot. Add the tuna burgers, reduce the heat to medium, and cook turning once, for 2 minutes on each side, or until golden brown. Take care not to overcook – the tuna should be medium rare.

4 Put a slice of tomato on the bottom half of the squares of focaccia, top with the tuna burger, and spread the cabbage tzatziki over the tuna. Cover with the tops of the focaccia and serve.

Cabbage tzatziki
200ml natural Greek yogurt
3 garlic cloves
juice of 1 lime
2 tbsp chopped fresh dill
1 tbsp chopped fresh flat-leaf parsley
150g thinly sliced napa cabbage (Chinese cabbage)
sea salt

• Combine the yogurt, garlic, lime juice, dill and parsley in a food processor or blender and process until smooth.
• Put the cabbage in a bowl, add the yogurt mixture, toss to coat.
• Season with sea salt to taste.

TO SERVE · 4 SMALL SQUARES FOCACCIA BREAD OR SMALL SOFT ROLLS · 4 SLICES TOMATO · CABBAGE TZATZIKI

Teriyaki-glazed tuna burger with shiso–seaweed salad

Another great flavoured tuna burger recipe to enjoy. I adore the salty, sweet Asian flavours which are both warm and delicately sweet. The seaweed can be purchased from Asian stores, usually salted it needs to be soaked before use.

700g fresh, skinless tuna steak
2 spring onions, finely chopped
½ garlic clove, crushed
1 tsp Chinese or Dijon mustard
1cm piece root ginger, grated
2 tbsp chopped fresh coriander
salt and freshly ground black pepper
vegetable or sunflower oil for cooking

FOR THE GLAZE
60ml teriyaki sauce
2 tbsp honey
2.5cm piece root ginger, grated
2 tsp rice wine vinegar

1 Cut the tuna into very small cubes or whiz quickly in a food processor. Add the spring onions, garlic, mustard, ginger, coriander, and whiz again briefly. Season lightly with salt and pepper. Transfer to a bowl and cover with clingfilm, chill for 1 hour.
2 Mix all the ingredients for the glaze together in a bowl.
3 Divide the mix into 8 evenly sized burgers.
4 Heat a thin film of oil in a large nonstick frying pan and, when hot, add the burgers and cook for 3–4 minutes on each side, keeping them medium rare, and brushing regularly with the glaze.
5 Toast the baps. Top the bases with the burgers, and then with the shiso–seaweed salad, close the baps and serve.

Shiso–seaweed salad

2 tbsp lime juice
½ small green chilli, thinly sliced
1 tbsp sugar
1 tbsp light soy sauce
12 slices pickled ginger
1cm piece root ginger, finely grated
1 tbsp chopped fresh coriander
4 tbsp peanut oil or vegetable oil
75g wakame seaweed, soaked in water for 2 hours, drained, dried
50g cucumber, thinly sliced
2 spring onions, thinly shredded lengthways
50g frisee lettuce
40g shiso cress or mustard cress
salt and freshly ground black pepper

• In a bowl mix the lime juice, chilli, sugar, soy sauce, ginger and coriander together. Add the oil and leave to infuse the flavours for 20 minutes.
• Place the seaweed, cucumber and spring onions in a bowl. Strain the dressing over, toss together well, and marinate for 1 hour at room temperature.
• To serve, add the frisee and shiso cress, toss lightly together, season and serve immediately.

TO SERVE • 8 MINI BURGER BAPS WITH BLACK SESAME SEEDS, SPLIT (SEE PAGE 135) • SHISO–SEAWEED SALAD

Piri piri tuna burger with grilled aubergines, spicy tomato relish and almond picada

Piri piri chillies were originally brought to Portugal from the Americas. The Portuguese then took them to Mozambique where they were named piri piri - a Swahili name meaning 'pepper pepper'. They are very hot and need to be used sparingly.

600g skinless, boneless yellow fin tuna
  steak
1 garlic clove, crushed
1 tsp piri piri sauce or hot pepper sauce
2 tbsp chopped fresh oregano
1 tbsp chopped fresh coriander
30ml olive oil
1 tsp freshly squeezed lemon juice
salt and freshly ground black pepper
pinch of paprika

1 Place the tuna steak in a food processor and whiz to a coarse purée or chop by hand.
2 In a large bowl, place the tuna, garlic, chilli sauce, herbs, 5ml of the olive oil, and lemon juice; season with salt, pepper and paprika, cover with clingfilm and chill for 1 hour.
3 Divide the mix into 4 evenly sized burgers.
4 Heat the remaining olive oil in a large nonstick frying pan, add the burgers and cook for 2 minutes on each side until golden brown. Take care not to overcook the tuna, it should be medium rare.
5 Toast the baps, dress the bases with some salad leaves and 2 slices grilled aubergine. Place a dollop of spicy tomato relish on top, followed by the tuna burgers.
6 Finally, top each burger with almond picada, close the baps and serve.

Grilled aubergines
60ml olive oil
1 large aubergine, cut into 1cm
  thick slices
sea salt and freshly ground black
  pepper
• Heat a pan grill with the olive oil, when hot add the aubergine slices and grill for 3–4 minutes on each side until soft and golden in colour, season to taste and serve.

Almond picada
1 garlic clove, peeled
4 tbsp whole blanched almonds,
  lightly toasted
½ red chilli, deseeded
15g fresh flat-leaf parsley
60ml good quality mayonnaise
1 tsp freshly squeezed lemon
  juice
• Place the garlic clove, toasted almonds, chilli and parsley in a mortar and pestle, grind to a fine paste.
• Add the mayonnaise, lemon juice, season to taste and serve.

TO SERVE • 4 BURGER BAPS, SPLIT • MIXED SALAD LEAVES • 8 SLICES GRILLED AUBERGINE • SPICY TOMATO RELISH (SEE PAGE 128) • ALMOND PICADA

Artichoke escalivada

2 red peppers, deseeded, cut into
  quarters
1 yellow pepper, deseeded, cut into
  quarters
½ aubergine, cut into 1cm slices
75ml olive oil
75g baby artichokes in oil, drained,
  halved
50g sunblush tomatoes in oil, drained
1 tbsp balsamic vinegar
1 tbsp chopped fresh flat-leaf parsley
1 garlic clove, crushed
1 tsp lemon juice
1 tsp pine nuts, toasted

• Preheat a grill at its highest setting.
Arrange the peppers and aubergine
slices on a grill pan, drizzle with the
olive oil, and grill until the skins are
charred and tender.
• Remove the peppers to a bowl and
cover with a plate or clingfilm to steam
for 5 minutes.
• Remove the cover and, when cool,
peel them to remove the skins. Cut the
peppers into strips.
• Place the pepper strips, aubergine
slices and remaining ingredients in a
bowl, toss together and serve.

Smoked paprika–sherry mayo

100ml good quality mayonnaise
  (see page 126)
2 tsp smoked paprika
1 tsp sherry vinegar
pinch of salt
• Mix all the ingredients together,
seasoning to taste.

Swordfish burger with artichoke escalivada and smoked paprika–sherry mayo

Swordfish is more identified with the Mediterranean than Britain, but it is becoming more widely available from
good supermarkets or fresh fishmongers. Like tuna it is very nutritious and extremely lean. When cooking these
burgers, do not let them get too hot or overcook them or they become dry.

600g skinless, boneles, good quality fresh
  swordfish fillet
25g ground almonds
juice and zest of ½ lemon
1 garlic clove, crushed
60ml good quality mayonnaise (page 126)
100g fresh white breadcrumbs
salt
pinch of white cayenne
vegetable oil for cooking

TO COAT BURGERS
25g plain flour
1 egg, lightly beaten
50g panko crumbs or fresh white
  breadcrumbs

1 Chop the swordfish finely, add the almonds, lemon juice and zest, and
  garlic. Add the mayonnaise and breadcrumbs to bind. Season with salt
  and white cayenne to taste. Shape the mix into 8 evenly sized patties.
2 Coat the burgers: pass the patties through the flour, then the egg and
  finally the panko crumbs. Chill for 30 minutes before cooking.
3 Heat a thin film of oil in a frying pan, suitable for the oven.
4 Cook the burgers gently for 4–5 minutes on each side, remove and
  drain on kitchen paper.
5 Toast the baps under a hot grill until golden if using.
6 Serve with artichoke escalivada, some patatas con ajo and with a bowl
  of smoked paprika–sherry mayo on the side.

TO SERVE · 4 BURGER BAPS, SPLIT (OPTIONAL) · ARTICHOKE ESCALIVADA
· PATATAS CON AJO (SEE PAGE 139) · SMOKED PAPRIKA–SHERRY MAYO

TO SERVE · 4 BABY BAGUETTES OR SMALL CRUSTY ROLLS
· CREOLE RÉMOULADE SLAW (SEE PAGE 133)
· TWICE-COOKED JACKET POTATOES (SEE PAGE 139)

New Orleans po'boy with Creole rémoulade slaw and twice-cooked jacket potatoes

200g skinless, boneless white fish fillet
  (e.g. cod, haddock or turbot), cut into
  chunks
450g tiger prawns, shelled, deveined
1 egg white
salt and freshly ground black pepper
3 spring onions, finely chopped
2 tbsp chopped fresh basil
½ tsp Creole or Dijon mustard
1 tsp Worcestershire sauce
pinch of cayenne
vegetable or sunflower oil for cooking

1 Place the fish with 100g of the prawns, the egg white, and a little salt in the food processor, and whiz for 20 seconds

2 Add the onions, basil and mustard, then whiz again for 5 seconds. Transfer to a bowl and mix in the Worcestershire sauce.

3 Chop the remaining tiger prawns in 0.5cm dice and add to the bowl. Adjust the seasoning with salt, pepper and cayenne; chill in the refrigerator for 2 hours.

4 Using wet hands, divide the mix into 4 equal amounts and roll each into a 2cm thick burger 12.5cm in length, big enough to fill the baguettes.

5 Heat a chargrill or pan grill until hot, brush the grill with some oil. Add the burgers and grill for 4–5 minutes, turning them regularly until golden and cooked through.

6 Reheat the baby baguettes in the oven; slit down one side with a sharp knife and prize open the baguette, taking care not to split it.

7 Fill with the Creole rémoulade slaw and top with the fish burgers; serve with the twice-cooked jacket potatoes.

Cod burger bocadillo with tomato and olive pesto, caper-saffron mayo

1 tbsp olive oil

2 shallots, finely chopped

400g skinless, boneless, firm white cod
   fillet

4 sea scallops

1 egg yolk

2 tbsp chopped fresh flat-leaf parsley

juice and zest of ¼ lemon

salt and freshly ground black pepper

pinch of paprika

flour for dusting

100g panko crumbs

vegetable or sunflower
   oil for cooking

25g unsalted butter

1 In a frying pan, heat the olive oil, add the shallots and cook for 3–4 minutes until softened and tender; remove and allow to cool.

2 Place the shallots, cod fillet, scallop meat, egg yolk and parsley in a food processor. Add the lemon juice and zest, along with a little salt, pepper and paprika. Whiz to a chunky paste – do not let it become too smooth – for about 20 seconds.

3 Using floured hands, divide the mix into 4 evenly sized burgers, then pass each burger through the beaten egg wash, then through the panko crumbs.

4 Pat into shape and to release any excess crumbs, chill for 30 minutes.

5 Heat a nonstick frying pan with a film of oil, add the burger and the butter and fry for 4–5 minutes each side until golden and crisp.

6 Top the bases with the tomato and olive pesto, then top with a cod burger. Serve with some dressed salad, the caper–saffron mayo and chickpea fries.

TO SERVE · 4 SMALL BAGUETTES OR ENGLISH MUFFINS, SPLIT · TOMATO AND OLIVE PESTO (SEE PAGE 126)
· CRISP GREEN SALAD DRESSED IN FRENCH DRESSING
· CAPER–SAFFRON MAYO (SEE PAGE 126)
· CHICKPEA FRIES (SEE PAGE 140)

Olive couscous salad

100g couscous
150ml hot chicken stock
½ yellow pepper, halved,
  deseeded, finely chopped
½ green pepper, halved,
  deseeded, finely chopped
1 garlic clove, crushed
75g green olives, pitted, chopped
60ml olive oil
2 tbsp chopped fresh flat-leaf
  parsley
juice of ½ lemon
½ tsp ground cumin

• Place the couscous in a bowl, pour the chicken stock over, cover with clingflm, and leave for 5–6 minutes until the couscous swells.
• Remove the clingfilm, fluff up with a fork, cover again and leave for a further 5 minutes.
• Add the peppers, garlic, olives to the couscous, mix well.
• Add the olive oil, parsley, lemon juice and cumin, toss well together and serve.

Jumbo prawn burger with North African spices, tomato chermoula, and olive couscous salad

In this recipe, marinating the fish really pays dividends, but ensure that the excess liquid is drained off or it will make the mix too soft. The traditional Moroccan chermoula is served with all manner of grilled foods especially fish – this is a great variation.

350g skinless, boneless, white fish fillet
  (e.g. cod, haddock, halibut)
250g jumbo tiger prawns, shelled,
  deveined
1 small garlic clove, crushed
1 tsp freshly squeezed lemon juice
½ tsp ground cumin
¼ tsp sweet paprika
¼ tsp powdered saffron
¼ tsp ground ginger
1 egg, beaten
1 tbsp chopped fresh coriander
1 tbsp chopped fresh flat-leaf parsley
salt and freshly ground black pepper
vegetable or sunflower oil for cooking

1 Cut the fish and prawns into large pieces, place in a bowl.
2 Add the garlic, lemon juice, cumin, paprika, saffron and ginger and mix well; leave to marinate for 10 minutes.
3 Drain off any excess liquid, then place in a food processor and whiz to a coarse paste. Transfer to a bowl, add the egg, herbs, salt and pepper, and mix well; chill for 1 hour.
4 Divide the mix into 8 evenly sized burgers.
5 Heat a thin film of oil in a large frying pan and, when hot, add the burgers and cook for 2–3 minutes on each side until golden. Remove and drain on kitchen paper.
6 Toast the baps. Mix the mayonnaise with the lettuce leaves, and place on the burger bases. Top with a burger, a few more leaves, then the second burger. Add a good dollop of tomato chermoula and close the lid. Serve with the olive couscous salad.

TO SERVE • 2 BURGER BAPS, SPLIT • 60ML GOOD QUALITY MAYONNAISE
• 50G BABY RED CHARD LEAVES • TOMATO CHERMOULA • OLIVE COUSCOUS SALAD

Tomato chermoula

1 tsp cumin seeds
½ tsp coriander seeds
150g canned plum tomatoes
1 garlic clove, crushed
1 small red chilli, deseeded, finely chopped
1 tbsp tomato purée
juice of ½ lemon
½ tsp ground sweet paprika

· Heat a dry frying pan over a high heat.
· Dry toast the cumin and coriander seeds for 10 seconds until they release their fragrance.
· Place in a mortar and pestle and crush until fine.
· Place in the blender, add remaining ingredients and whiz to a paste. Keep refrigerated until required.

Hot peanut–mint dip

150g smooth or chunky peanut
butter
100ml water
2 tbsp Asian sweet chilli sauce
1 garlic clove, crushed
2.5cm piece root ginger
juice of 1 lime
1 tsp soy sauce
2 tbsp chopped fresh mint
• In a blender, whiz all the
ingredients except the mint to a
smooth purée. Add the mint just
before serving.

Thai lobster and lemongrass sticks

with hot peanut–mint dip (makes 12)

These delicious little patties, cooked on their lemongrass sticks, really do make an
impressive talking point, served with Champagne of course! The perfect prelude to a meal.

14 lemongrass sticks
450g cleaned lobster or king prawns, deveined
125g skinless, boneless white fish fillet
4 spring onions
3 tbsp chopped fresh coriander
1 tbsp Thai fish sauce (nam pla)
2 tsp honey
2 garlic cloves, crushed
1 small egg white
1 tsp cornflour
1 tsp black sesame seeds
vegetable or sunflower oil for cooking

1 Remove the tough outer leaves of the lemongrass, chop 2 of them
   very finely; with the remaining 12, cut the tops off so that you
   have 15cm lengths with the thickest part intact.
2 In a blender, place the lobster meat, white fish, chopped lemongrass
   and the remaining ingredients, and whiz to a smooth paste.
3 Divide the mix into 12 x 4cm balls, using wet hands, then mould
   over the thick ends of the lemongrass sticks; chill in the refrigerator
   for 1 hour.
4 Sprinkle lightly with sesame seeds, then brush with a little oil; grill
   or panfry for 4–6 minutes, until golden. Serve the dip separately.

TO SERVE • HOT PEANUT–MINT DIP

Niçoise crab burger with fennel escabèche and sundried pepper rouille

400g skinless, boneless, firm white fish
   fillet (e.g. sole or halibut)
salt and freshly ground black pepper
200g freshly picked white crabmeat
30ml good quality mayonnaise
2 tbsp freshly chopped flat-leaf parsley
¼ tsp Dijon mustard
zest of ¼ lemon
100g fresh white breadcrumbs
vegetable or sunflower oil for cooking
25g unsalted butter

1 Place the white fish in a food processor with a little salt and whiz to a coarse pulp. Transfer to a bowl and incorporate the crabmeat, mayonnaise, parsley, mustard and lemon zest; mix well. Add the breadcrumbs, mix again and season to taste.

2 Divide the mix into 4 evenly sized burgers.

3 Heat a thin film of oil in a nonstick frying pan, add the burgers and the butter and fry until golden and cooked through, about 4 minutes each side.

4 Cut the muffins in half, allowing half per person.

5 Place some fennel escabèche on each base, topped with the rocket leaves.

6 Place a burger on top, and garnish with a good dollop of sundried pepper rouille.

TO SERVE · 2 ENGLISH MUFFINS, SPLIT · ROCKET LEAVES · FENNEL ESCABÈCHE · SUNDRIED PEPPER ROUILLE (SEE PAGE 125)

Fennel escabèche
1 large head fennel, peeled
30ml lemon juice
60ml olive oil
salt and freshly ground pepper
· Using a potato peeler, thinly shave or slice the fennel wafer thin. Place in a bowl, add the lemon juice, olive oil, salt and pepper and leave to marinate for 4 hours before use.

Asian crab burger with sweet chilli ketchup and yuzu crème fraîche

175g skinless, boneless white fish fillet
(e.g. cod, haddock, etc.)
2 garlic cloves, crushed
1 tbsp Thai fish sauce (nam pla)
½ tbsp ketchup manis (Indonesian soy
sauce)
½ tbsp oyster sauce
350g fresh white crabmeat
1 small egg, beaten
30g unsweetened, desiccated coconut
1 red chilli, deseeded, finely chopped
4 spring onions, thinly sliced
4 tbsp chopped fresh coriander
salt and freshly ground black pepper
vegetable or sunflower oil for cooking

1 Place the white fish fillet in a food processor, add the garlic, fish sauce, ketchup manis, oyster sauce, and process for a few seconds until it forms a coarse paste.
2 Dry the crabmeat on a cloth, squeeze out any excess moisture and add to the fish. Add the egg and process once more.
3 Transfer the mixture to a bowl, add the coconut, chilli, spring onions and coriander. Season with salt and pepper.
4 Divide the mix into 8 evenly sized burgers. Heat a thin film of the oil in a frying pan, add the burgers and cook for 3–4 minutes until golden.
5 Toast the baps. Top the bases with shredded lettuce and slices of cucumber. Place some sweet chilli ketchup on top, then top each with a burger. Repeat with a little more lettuce, cucumber, ketchup then another burger. Finish with a dollop of yuzu crème fraîche, close the baps and serve.

Yuzu crème fraîche
100ml crème fraîche
3 tbsp bottled yuzu juice
(available from Asian stores)
2 tbsp chopped fresh mint
1 tbsp chopped fresh coriander
salt and freshly ground black
pepper
· Mix all the ingredients together,
season to taste.

TO SERVE · BURGER BAPS, SPLIT · 50G SHREDDED ICEBERG LETTUCE · 50G THINLY SLICED
CUCUMBER · SWEET CHILLI KETCHUP (SEE PAGE 125)

Devilled scallop burger with portobello mushrooms, mustard hollandaise and thyme-grilled corn

I find that freshly caught scallop is the finest and most delicate of all molluscs. Scallops also make incredibly good and juicy burgers despite their low fat content. When cooking them take great care not to overcook them – the centre should be barely cooked.

250g skinless, boneless lemon sole fillet
400g cleaned sea scallops, roe removed
salt and freshly ground black pepper
30g fresh white breadcrumbs
25g chopped fresh flat-leaf parsley
1 egg white
vegetable or sunflower oil for cooking
good pinch of cayenne

1 Place the lemon sole fillet in a food processor with half the scallops and a little salt. Add the breadcrumbs and parsley and whiz to a fine paste.

2 Take the remaining scallops and chop them roughly, add to the sole and process for 20 seconds or until just blended: there should be small lumps of scallops in the mixture. Add the egg white and whiz to mix, still keeping the mixture slightly chunky in texture. Season to taste with salt and pepper.

3 Using oiled hands, shape the mixture into burgers, place on a plate, cover and refrigerate until ready to cook.

4 Heat a thin film of oil in a large nonstick frying pan and, when hot, remove the burgers from the refrigerator and dust them all over with a little cayenne pepper.

5 Cook the burgers for 4–5 minutes on each side until golden; they should remain a little undercooked in the centre to keep them juicy and moist.

6 Place the grilled portobello mushrooms on 4 serving plates, top each with a slice of tomato and then with a scallop burger.

7 Coat each burger with some mustard hollandaise, garnish with the watercress, grilled bacon and thyme-grilled corn.

Grilled portobello mushrooms

45ml vegetable oil
4 portobello mushrooms, stems removed, peeled
salt and freshly ground black pepper

• Heat a pan or chargrill until hot, brush with the vegetable oil and cook the mushrooms for 6–8 minutes until charred all over; season to taste.

Mustard hollandaise

75ml white wine vinegar
1 tsp crushed black peppercorns
4 egg yolks
150g unsalted butter, clarified, hot
juice of ¼ lemon
2 tsp Dijon mustard

• Place the vinegar in a small pan with 2 tbsp cold water and the peppercorns. Bring to the boil for 30 seconds, then strain into a heatproof bowl, cool slightly.
• Place the bowl over a pan of boiling water, and whisk in the egg yolks until they double in volume and become opaque in colour.
• Add the hot clarified butter in a thin stream and whisk until thickened. Add the lemon juice and mustard and keep the sauce warm, but do not let it get too hot or the sauce will separate.

Thyme-grilled corn

3 corn on the cob, husks removed
60ml vegetable oil
75g unsalted butter
2 tsp freshly picked thyme leaves
salt and freshly ground black pepper

• Blanch the corn in boiling water for 10 minutes, remove and cut in 4cm chunks.
• Brush with the oil, heat a chargrill or grill pan until hot, grill for 10 minutes until lightly charred, turning them often.
• Heat the butter with the thyme in a pan for 2 minutes, pour over the grilled corn, season and serve.

TO SERVE • GRILLED PORTOBELLO MUSHROOMS • 4 THICK SLICES BEEF TOMATOES • MUSTARD HOLLANDAISE
• 50G WATERCRESS • 8 RASHERS STREAKY BACON, GRILLED • THYME-GRILLED CORN

Walnut, courgette
and millet burger

VEGETARIAN

Walnut, courgette and millet burger

with lemon mint labna and smoky tomato and pepper relish

1 courgette, grated
salt and freshly ground black pepper
½ tsp curry powder
⅛ tsp turmeric
100g millet
2 tbsp vegetable oil
1 onion, finely chopped
100g flat mushrooms, finely chopped
150g walnuts, finely ground
50g fresh white breadcrumbs
1 egg, beaten

Lemon mint labna
1 egg white
100ml Greek yogurt, thick variety or well
  drained
zest of ¼ lemon
• Whisk the egg white until stiff, then fold in the
yogurt to combine, add the lemon zest,
seasoning lightly, and serve.

1 Place the grated courgette on a tray, sprinkle liberally with salt and leave for 25 minutes to extract the moisture. Rinse under cold water, squeeze dry in your hands and dry in a towel.
2 In a pan, bring 300ml water to the boil with the curry, turmeric and a little salt. Add the millet, simmer gently for 15–20 minutes over a low heat, until the millet has absorbed all the water. Transfer to a bowl, leave to go cold.
3 Heat the oil in a nonstick frying pan, add the onion and cook until soft and tender. Add the grated courgette and mushroom and cook for 5 minutes until soft.
4 In a bowl, mix the ground walnuts, cooked millet, breadcrumbs with the vegetables. Add the beaten egg and mix to a paste. Season with pepper to taste.
5 Place in the refrigerator to chill for 1 hour, then shape into 4 evenly sized burgers.
6 Lay some dressed salad leaves on the half potatoes, top with some smoky red-pepper relish. Place a burger on each, then top with a good dollop of lemon mint labna, close with the potato lid and serve.

TO SERVE · 4 JACKET POTATOES, SPLIT · MIXED SALAD LEAVES, DRESSED IN FRENCH DRESSING · SMOKY TOMATO AND PEPPER RELISH (SEE PAGE 130) · LEMON MINT LABNA

Vegetarian feta club burger with coriander–avocado pesto, slow dried tomatoes, olive mayo

1 onion, firmly chopped
120g feta cheese, crumbled
1 tbsp chopped fresh mint
125g fresh white breadcrumbs
3 tbsp chickpea flour (gram flour)
1 large egg
salt and freshly ground black pepper
vegetable or sunflower oil for cooking

Coriander–avocado pesto
100g picked fresh coriander leaves
1 garlic clove, crushed
1 avocado, stone removed
2 tbsp freshly grated Parmesan cheese
2 tbsp pine nuts, toasted
100ml extra-virgin olive oil
• Place the coriander leaves and garlic in a
blender, add the avocado flesh, Parmesan and
pine nuts and whiz to a purée; using the feed
tube at the top of the blender, slowly drizzle in
the olive oil to form a sauce. Season to taste.

1 Place the onion in a bowl, add the crumbled feta, mint, breadcrumbs and chickpea flour. Add the egg, season to taste, and bind together, chill the mix for 30 minutes, then shape into 8 small fairly flat shaped burgers.
2 Heat a film of oil in a nonstick frying pan, add the burgers and fry gently for 3–4 minutes on each side, remove and keep them warm.
3 Take 4 slices of the sour dough bread, and spread liberally with the olive mayo. Top each with some iceberg and rocket leaves, followed by a burger.
4 Top with slow dried tomatoes, a layer of sliced egg, then a good dollop of the coriander–avocado pesto.
5 Top with a second slice of bread and repeat the layers again.
6 Finish with the last slice of bread, then press gently down to compress the filling within. Cut into 2 halves and enjoy!

TO SERVE · 12 THIN SLICES SOUR DOUGH BREAD · ICEBERG LETTUCE · 50G ROCKET LEAVES · SLOW DRIED TOMATOES · 2 HARD BOILED EGGS, PEELED, SLICED · OLIVE MAYO (SEE PAGE 126) · CORIANDER–AVOCADO PESTO

Slow-dried tomatoes
8 ripe but firm plum tomatoes,
  cut in half horizontally
1 garlic clove, crushed
1 tbsp picked fresh thyme
  leaves
½ tsp castor sugar
coarse sea salt, freshly ground
  pepper
60ml olive oil
• Preheat the oven to
200°C/Gas 6. Place the
tomatoes on a baking tray, cut
side up, scatter over and rub on
the garlic, thyme leaves, sugar,
salt and pepper. Finally, drizzle
the oil over, place in the oven to
bake until very soft and
shrivelled. Leave to cool. These
keep in olive oil for up to a week
in the refrigerator.

Grilled aubergine, goats' cheese and sunblush-tomato burger

This recipe is from talented chef and friend Peter Gordon, the man said to have brought 'fusion' cooking to Britain. Peter is consultant to Gourmet Burger Kitchen, a themed burger restaurant group serving wonderful burger creations throughout London; he recommends sour dough baps if you can find them.

4 x 1.5cm slices firm chèvre (goats' cheese) log
3 tbsp flour
salt and freshly ground black pepper
1 egg, beaten for egg wash
75g panko crumbs mixed with 1 tbsp honey
vegetable or sunflower oil for deep frying
8 x 1cm thick slices aubergine
olive oil for brushing

Balsamic vinaigrette
1 tbsp balsamic vinegar
4 tbsp extra-virgin olive oil
salt and freshly ground black pepper
· Whisk ingredients together ready for serving.

1 Coat the goats' cheese slices as follows: dust the slices of cheese with the flour, mixed with a little salt and pepper. Dip them in to the eggwash and then into the panko crumbs.

2 Press the panko into the goats' cheese firmly. Dip again into the egg wash and then again into the panko. It is important to double coat to prevent the cheese oozing into the fryer oil. Chill in the refrigerator for at least 30 minutes.

3 Heat the oil in a deep fat fryer or large saucepan to 180°C.

4 Heat a cast iron pan grill until very hot, brush the aubergine slices with olive oil and grill them until cooked to a golden colour, about 3 minutes each side.

5 Fry the goats' cheese burgers for 3–4 minutes until golden, then drain well on kitchen paper. Toast the burger baps on both sides.

6 Assemble the burgers: spread the bap bases with the mayonnaise, then top each with 2 slices of aubergine, then with the sunblush tomatoes.

7 Place a goats' cheese burger on top, then the cooked tomato relish, a few salad leaves dressed in a little balsamic vinaigrette, and close the lid. If you like, serve with long satay sticks to keep them from toppling over. Serve with more relish alongside.

TO SERVE · 4 PLAIN OR SOUR DOUGH BURGER BAPS, SPLIT (PAGE 135)
· 75G SUNBLUSH TOMATOES IN OIL, DRAINED · 100G MIXED SALAD LEAVES
· BALSAMIC VINAIGRETTE · 60ML GOOD QUALITY MAYONNAISE
· 60ML COOKED TOMATO RELISH (SEE PAGE 129)

Pumpkin couscous burger in pittas with pomegranate–herb chilli yogurt

In this burger recipe the squash adds a nutty sweetness and, when mixed with delicate spices and fluffy couscous, makes an interesting flavour-packed veggi burger. Prepare this wonderful yogurt-based dip to serve when pomegranates are available!

300g wedge pumpkin or butternut squash

1 large potato, washed

250g couscous, cooked to package instructions

100g currants

1 onion, finely chopped

75g walnuts, finely chopped

2 tsp ground cumin

1 tsp ground cinnamon

1 tsp ground allspice

2 eggs, beaten

1 Preheat the oven to 200°C/Gas 6.

2 Place the pumpkin and the potato on a baking tray and place in the oven to bake. Remove the pumpkin after 30 minutes, leave the potato for a further 30 minutes or longer depending on the size of the potato.

3 When both are cooked, allow to cool. Peel the potato and remove the skin from the pumpkin. Place the flesh in a large bowl, and mash to a coarse purée.

4 Add the couscous, currants, onion, walnuts and spices and bind together with the eggs. Shape the mix into 8 x 10cm sausage-like burgers.

5 Cook the burgers on a chargrill or in a nonstick frying pan until cooked and golden.

6 Open up the pitta breads, fill each with shredded lettuce, cucumber slices and 2 pumpkin burgers. Serve the pomegranate–herb chilli yogurt on the side.

Pomegranate–herb chilli yogurt

150ml natural thick-set Greek yogurt
3 spring onions, finely chopped
1 green chilli, finely chopped
½ garlic clove, crushed
1 tsp white wine vinegar
salt
1 tbsp chopped fresh dill
1 tbsp chopped fresh mint
1 fresh pomegranate, halved, seeds removed
1 tbsp pomegranate molasses (optional)

• If the yogurt is not thick you will have to line a colander with cheesecloth, place over a bowl, add the yogurt, and let it drain for at least 5 minutes, preferably overnight.
• In a bowl mix the thick yogurt with the spring onions, chilli, garlic and vinegar, season with salt. Add the herbs. Squeeze out the seeds from the pomegranate halves and add them with the molasses if using.
• Serve chilled.

Roasted vegetable and kasha falafel burger with smoky corn relish

You'll find kasha (roasted buckwheat groats) in most health food stores – I love kasha made into falafel-style burgers and even big meat lovers will find they make vegetarian eating a real pleasure. Char the corn cobs on the grill for a wonderful smoky relish.

90g whole grain kasha (roasted buckwheat groats)

1 egg

10g unsalted butter

1 onion, finely diced

1 carrot, peeled, finely diced

1 courgette, finely diced

2 garlic cloves, crushed

400g cooked chickpeas (canned are fine, well drained)

2 spring onions, finely chopped

2 tbsp chopped fresh coriander

2 tbsp plain flour

2 tsp ground cumin

¼ tsp baking powder

salt, freshly ground black pepper and cayenne pepper

vegetable oil for deep frying

1 Place the kasha and egg in a small bowl and leave to stand for 10 minutes.

2 Melt the butter in a frying pan over moderate heat. Add the vegetables and garlic and fry for 8 minutes until soft. Add the kasha and fry for 3–4 minutes until the kasha is golden.

3 Add 300ml water, bring to the boil, season with a little salt, cover and simmer for 15–20 minutes, until the kasha is tender and all the water absorbed, remove and cool.

4 To make the falafel, place the kasha, vegetables and remaining ingredients in a blender and whiz to form a moist paste, season to taste. Form into 8 x 5cm diameter patties.

5 Place the vegetable oil in a deep fat fryer or deep saucepan and heat it to 180°C. Fry the kasha falafel in batches until golden brown, about 2 minutes; drain on kitchen paper and keep them warm.

6 Toast the burger baps, place a good dollop of corn relish on the base bap, followed by a falafel burger, some salad leaves and a slice of beetroot. Finish with the remaining falafel burger and close the lid. Serve the lemon mint labna alongside.

Smoky corn relish

3 corn on the cob, husks removed

175ml white wine vinegar

75g sugar

1 garlic clove, crushed

2.5cm piece root ginger, finely grated

½ tsp ground allspice

¼ tsp dried mustard powder

4 spring onions, white part only, finely chopped

1 red pepper, halved, deseeded, finely chopped

1 small red chilli, deseeded, finely chopped

1 tsp cornstarch mixed with 1 tsp of cold water

salt and freshly ground black pepper

• Blanch the cobs in boiling water for 2–3 minutes, remove, drain.

• Heat a chargrill or pan grill until very hot. Add the cobs and grill for 5–6 minutes, turning them, until lightly charred all over.

• When cool enough to handle, run a small knife along the length of the cob to remove the kernels.

• In a pan, bring to the boil the vinegar, sugar, add the garlic, ginger and spices, cook for 10–15 minutes.

• Add the corn, spring onions, pepper and chilli and cook for a further 6–8 minutes. Stir in the cornstarch, cook for 30 seconds, season to taste and cool.

• Refrigerate for at least 2 days before serving; it will keep in the refrigerator for up to 5 days.

TO SERVE · 4 SESAME BURGER BAPS, SPLIT · 50G GREEN SALAD LEAVES · 4 THICK SLICES COOKED BEETROOT
· SMOKY CORN RELISH · 75ML LEMON MINT LABNA (SEE PAGE 106)

The spa burger with mango–alfalfa sprouts, and red pepper and cashew tarator

I created this cheeseburger for the newly built spa complex at the hotel, to serve to our guests as they were being pampered. Cottage cheese, spinach and wheatgerm, offset by a nutty red-pepper sauce and delicate alfalfa sprouts, tempts the most jaded palates.

olive oil for frying
1 onion, finely chopped
1 garlic clove, crushed
100g cooked spinach
125g cottage cheese, well drained
100g fresh white breadcrumbs
100g wheatgerm, lightly toasted
50g ground walnuts
2 tbsp chopped fresh mint
1 egg
salt and freshly ground black pepper
pinch of cayenne

1 Heat a little oil in a nonstick frying pan, add the onion, garlic, and cook until softened.
2 Squeeze the cooked spinach in a clean cloth to remove all the excess moisture, finally chop it and add to the pan. Transfer the contents of the pan to a bowl, add the remaining ingredients, binding with the egg. Season to taste.
3 Divide the mix into 4 evenly sized burgers.
4 Heat a thin film of the oil in a nonstick frying pan, add the burgers and cook for 3–4 minutes on each side until golden.
5 Toast the burger baps, spread some red pepper and cashew tarator on the bases then top with the burgers. Finally add a heap of alfalfa sprout slaw on top, close the bap and serve with a fresh green salad.

TO SERVE · 4 SESAME BURGER BAPS, SPLIT · MANGO–ALFALFA SPROUTS · RED PEPPER AND CASHEW TARATOR · GREEN SALAD

Mango–alfalfa sprouts
75g alfalfa sprouts
1 mango, finely shredded
50g fresh coriander leaves
2 tbsp maple syrup
1 small red onion, thinly sliced
2 tbsp olive oil
juice of 1 lime
· Toss all the ingredients together just before serving.

Red pepper and cashew tarator
75g fresh white breadcrumbs
90ml skimmed milk
50g roasted red peppers in oil, drained, oil reserved
50g cashew nuts
2 garlic cloves, crushed
salt and freshly ground black pepper
· Place the breadcrumbs in a bowl, pour the milk over and leave to soak for 10 minutes.
· Place the peppers, cashew nuts and garlic in a blender and whiz to a smooth purée.
· Squeeze out any excess moisture from the bread, add to the blender, and whiz again.
· Finally add 1 tbsp of the drained pepper oil. Season to taste. The tarator should be fairly thick in consistency, if not add a little more breadcrumbs.

Black bean koftas with corn and grilled-pineapple mojo

4 tbsp vegetable oil

3 spring onions, finely chopped

1 garlic clove, crushed

1 small green chilli, deseeded, finely chopped

350g cooked black beans

2 tsp Dijon mustard

2 tsp chickpea flour (gram flour)

4 tbsp chopped fresh coriander

½ tsp ground cumin

75g fresh white breadcrumbs

salt and freshly ground black pepper

100g feta cheese or other sharp cheese, cut into 1cm dice

1 Heat 2 tbsp of the oil in a pan, add the onions, garlic and chilli. Cook for 2 minutes.

2 Mash the cooked beans with the mustard, chickpea flour, coriander and cumin, and mix well. Add the breadcrumbs and cooked onion mix. Season to taste.

3 Shape the mix into small 3cm balls. With your finger make a small indentation in the centre of each ball, then fill each with some cheese. Cover over to secure the cheese filling.

4 Heat the remaining oil and fry the koftas for 3–4 minutes, keeping them moving.

5 Serve the cooked koftas in the prepared corn husks with the corn and grilled-pineapple mojo, garnished with fresh coriander leaves.

TO PREPARE THE CORN HUSKS

Soak the corn husks in hot water for 2 hours or until soft and pliable. Shake off the excess water. Take each husk and tear two thin strips off lengthways to make the ties. Roll up the larger part and fasten a tie 1cm from each end with a tight bow. Carefully open the centre to form a little boat shape.

TO SERVE • 4 DRIED CORN HUSKS (SEE ABOVE)
• CORN AND GRILLED-PINEAPPLE MOJO (SEE PAGE 131)
• FRESH CORIANDER LEAVES TO GARNISH

Turkistan chickpea burger with pistachio, beetroot and feta tabbouleh

2 tbsp olive oil

1 small onion, finely chopped

1 garlic clove, crushed

1 tsp ground cumin

90g cracked wheat (bulghur), soaked in boiling water for 20 minutes, then well drained

1 tbsp chopped fresh flat-leaf parsley

400g cooked chickpeas (canned are fine)

100g freshly grated Cheddar cheese

50g pine nuts, toasted

salt and freshly ground black pepper

vegetable or sunflower oil for cooking

1 Heat the olive oil in a frying pan, add the onion, garlic and cumin, and cook for 6–8 minutes until soft.

2 Add the cracked wheat and parsley and cook for 5 minutes longer.

3 Transfer to a food processor, add the remaining ingredients and whiz to a coarse paste.

4 Using wet hands, shape the mix into 4 evenly sized burgers, chill for 1 hour.

5 Heat a chargrill or pan grill with a little oil and, when hot, add the burgers and cook gently for 3–4 minutes each side.

6 Chargrill the pitta breads. Serve the burgers between the hot pitta breads and with the pistachio, beetroot and feta tabbouleh alongside.

TO SERVE • 8 MINI PITTA BREADS (SEE PAGE 135)
• PISTACHIO, BEETROOT AND FETA TABBOULEH (SEE PAGE 133)

Lentil nut koftas with rojal salsa and cumin naan bread

Indian cooking is renowned for its earthy lentil-based dishes. These lentil nut koftas are delicately spiced and made from the best Puy lentils. Everyone will adore them, especially when served with the fragrant sweet and sour rojal salsa. Utterly delicious!

Rojal salsa

1 tomato, chopped
1 shallot, cut into thin rings
2 spring onions, chopped
30g fresh pineapple, chopped
30g cucumber, chopped
2 tbsp peanut oil
2 tbsp maple syrup
1 tbsp lime pickle, chopped
1 tbsp unsweetened desiccated
   coconut
salt and freshly ground black
   pepper
• Mix all the ingredients together
in a bowl and leave to infuse for
1 hour before use.

Coriander raita

100ml natural yogurt
2 tbsp chopped fresh coriander
pinch of saffron
Mix all the ingredients together,
ready for use.

TO SERVE • 8 CUMIN NAAN BREADS (SEE PAGE 136)
• ROJAL SALSA • CORIANDER RAITA • MINT LEAVES TO GARNISH

60ml vegetable oil

1 onion

2 garlic cloves, crushed

1 green chilli, deseeded, finely chopped

1 tsp ground coriander

¼ tsp black mustard seeds

400g cooked Puy lentils

1 tbsp curry paste

25g ground almonds

50g salted almonds

1 small egg

4 tbsp chickpea flour (gram flour)

salt and freshly ground black pepper

8 bamboo or wooden skewers, soaked

1 Preheat the grill to its highest setting.

2 Heat 4cm oil in a frying pan and, when hot, add the onion, garlic, chilli, ground coriander and mustard seeds, cook for 2–3 minutes until the onion is soft and lightly golden.

3 Add the cooked lentils and cook for a further 2–3 minutes.

4 Add the curry paste and cook for a further 2 minutes.

5 Transfer to a food processor, add the almonds, egg and 3 tbsp of the flour and pulse until the mix comes together firmly. Season to taste.

6 Using 8 pre-soaked bamboo skewers and floured hands, mould the mix around the skewers to form a kofta sausage shape, 1–2.5cm thick. Place on a grill tray, brush with the remaining oil, and grill until golden, about 5 minutes, turning them regularly. Alternatively pan fry them in a nonstick pan.

7 Garnish the kofta burgers with mint leaves, and serve on the warm cumin naan breads, with bowls of rojal salsa and coriander raita alongside.

Quorn bruschetta with Moroccan-style caponata

vegetable or sunflower oil for cooking

1 onion, finely chopped

1 garlic clove, crushed

2.5cm piece ginger root, peeled, finely grated

½ tsp ground cumin

70g almonds

50g fresh white breadcrumbs

300g quorn mince

1 large egg

1 tbsp double cream

2 tbsp chopped fresh coriander

1 tbsp chopped fresh mint

salt and freshly ground black pepper

1 Heat a thin film of the oil in a nonstick frying pan, and add the onion, garlic, ginger and cumin; cook until soft, about 3–4 minutes, then add the almonds and breadcrumbs and cook for a further 2 minutes.

2 Transfer the mixture to a food processor, add the quorn mince and egg, and whiz to a coarse purée. Transfer to a bowl, add the cream, chopped coriander and mint. Season to taste.

3 Divide the mix into 4 evenly sized burgers.

4 Heat a thin film of oil in a nonstick frying pan, add the burgers, fry until golden on both sides and crisp.

5 Split the baguette in half lengthways and toast, top with some dressed salad leaves, then top each with some Moroccan-style caponata and a quorn burger, and serve immediately.

Moroccan-style caponata

¼ tsp cumin seeds

60ml olive oil

1 stick celery, peeled, thickly sliced

½ aubergine, cut into 1cm dice

1 small red pepper, halved, deseeded, cut into 1cm dice

1 onion, chopped

1 courgette cut in 1cm dice

8 green olives, pitted

1 garlic clove, crushed

¼ tsp paprika

¼ tsp ground cinnamon

2 tbsp balsamic vinegar

2 tbsp maple syrup

2 tbsp soaked raisins

• Heat a dry frying pan over a high heat, add the cumin seeds and quickly toast them to give off their fragrance. Remove to one side.

• Add the oil to the pan, add the vegetables, olives and garlic and fry for 6–8 minutes until slightly softened. Add the dry spices, the toasted cumin seeds, and cook for a further 2 minutes.

• Add the vinegar, syrup and raisins; cover with a lid, reduce the heat and cook until the vegetables are tender and syrupy in consistency.

• The caponata can be served cold or hot. I suggest hot for this burger. The caponata can be made up to 3 days in advance.

TO SERVE •1 X 12.5CM LENGTH BAGUETTE • GREEN SALAD LEAVES, DRESSED IN BALSAMIC DRESSING • MOROCCAN-STYLE CAPONATA

Southwest red-bean burger with green chilli mayo and three-onion ceviche

15ml olive oil

1 onion, finely chopped

1 garlic clove, crushed

1 tsp ground cumin

1 tsp ground coriander

¼ tsp turmeric

100g portobello mushrooms, finely chopped

400g cooked or canned red kidney beans

2 tbsp chopped fresh coriander

50g spicy tortilla chips, crushed

75g fresh white breadcrumbs

1 tbsp hot pepper sauce

salt and freshly ground black pepper

flour for dusting

vegetable oil for cooking

1 Heat the oil in a frying pan, add the onion and garlic, and cook until softened. Add the spices, mix well, and cook for a further 2 minutes. Add the mushrooms and cook over a low heat until they are soft but dry.

2 Place the beans in a bowl and mash lightly with a fork; add to the mushrooms along with the coriander, crushed tortilla chips, breadcrumbs and chilli sauce. Season to taste.

3 Using floured hands, form the mixture into 4 evenly sized burgers (if the mix is a little too wet, add more breadcrumbs). Brush the burgers with a little oil.

4 Heat a thin film of the oil in a large nonstick frying pan and, when hot, add the burgers. Cook for 2–3 minutes on each side until golden and crispy.

5 Toast the baps and top the bases with 2 slices of tomato, then a good dollop of green chilli mayonnaise, followed by a burger. Finish with the three-onion ceviche and close the bap.

Three-onion ceviche

juice of 1 lime

2 tbsp peanut oil

½ garlic clove, crushed

1 tbsp chopped fresh coriander

4 spring onions, shredded lengthways in 5cm lengths

1 red onion, halved, thinly sliced

2 tbsp chives, cut into 5cm lengths

salt and freshly ground black pepper

• In a bowl whisk together the lime juice, peanut oil and garlic, and add the coriander. Leave to marinate for 30 minutes. Just before serving, add the onions and chives, and toss gently together. Season to taste.

TO SERVE • 4 CHEESE BURGER BAPS, SPLIT (SEE PAGE 135)• 8 SLICES TOMATO • THREE-ONION CEVICHE • GREEN CHILLI MAYO (SEE PAGE 126)

Oven cheese fries

ALL THE SIDES

Sauces

Simple tomato ketchup

Simple tomato ketchup

30ml olive oil
2 onions, peeled, finely chopped
2 garlic cloves, crushed
4 x 400g cans peeled plum tomatoes, chopped
200g light brown sugar
150ml cider or white wine vinegar
2 tbsp tomato purée
2 tbsp black treacle or molasses
2 tsp dried mustard powder
5cm piece cinnamon stick
½ tsp ground coriander
¼ tsp dried chilli flakes
¼ tsp ground cloves
1 small bayleaf
juice of 2 limes

• Heat the oil in a heavy based pan, add the onions, garlic and cook for 5–6 minutes until softened but with no colour. Add all the remaining ingredients except the lime juice and bring to the boil.
• Reduce the heat to low and simmer the ketchup for 1–1¼ hours, stirring frequently.
• Pass the ketchup sauce through a medium strainer or food mill and return it to the pan.
• Cook over a low heat again for a further 30 minutes or so until the sauce is reduced and thickened in consistency.
• Allow to cool before stirring in the lime juice. Refrigerate until needed, it can be kept in a sealed container in the refrigerator for up to 5 days, longer in a sealed sterilised jar.

PG VARIATIONS

HORSERADISH KETCHUP
Add 1 tbsp freshly grated horseradish to the recipe during cooking.

CURRY KETCHUP
Add 2 tbsp curry paste to the cooked onion and garlic, cook for 5 minutes before adding the remaining ingredients.

SWEET CHILLI KETCHUP
Add 2 tbsp Asian sweet chilli sauce to the finished ketchup.

TABASCO–CUMIN KETCHUP
Replace the ground coriander in the recipe with 2 tbsp toasted and crushed cumin seeds, finish the ketchup with Tabasco sauce to taste.

Green tomato ketchup

A great way of using that glut of green tomatoes, both tasty and very economical, kept sterilised, it keeps for months and makes a refreshing change from the deep red variety.

3kg green tomatoes, roughly chopped
100g sea salt or coarse salt
30ml olive oil
4 onions, peeled, finely chopped
3 garlic cloves, crushed
700g brown sugar
600ml white wine vinegar or cider vinegar
2 tsp ground turmeric
1 tsp mustard seed
1 tsp celery seed
1 tsp ground ginger
1 tsp black peppercorns, finely crushed
1 tsp ground coriander

• Place the tomatoes in a large bowl, sprinkle with salt and leave to stand for 1 hour to release juices.
• Heat the oil in a heavy based saucepan, add the onions and garlic and cook for 5–6 minutes without colouring.
• Rinse the tomatoes under fresh cold water, drain well and add to the pan. Add all the remaining ingredients, and bring to the boil.
• Reduce the heat and simmer for 1 hour or until very soft and pulpy in consistency.
• Pass the mixture through a medium strainer or food mill, then return to the pan.
• Cook for a further 35 minutes until the tomatoes are reduced and thickened.
• Allow to cool and refrigerate until needed. To store longer, place the green tomato ketchup in a hot sterilised preserving jar.

Sundried pepper rouille

1 baking potato
60ml olive oil
1 garlic clove, crushed
50g sundried red peppers, chopped
1 egg yolk
salt and freshly ground black pepper
good pinch of cayenne

• Preheat the oven to 180°C/Gas 4.
• Place the potato on a baking tray, and bake in the oven for 1–1¼ hours or until soft; remove and cool slightly.
• Meanwhile warm the olive oil and garlic in a small pan, stir in the peppers, remove from the heat and leave to soften for 10–15 minutes.
• Cut the potato in half, then using a spoon, scoop out the inner flesh into a blender.
• Add the peppers and garlic oil and whiz to a thick purée. Finally add the egg yolk, salt and pepper and the cayenne to give a little heat.

Beb's barbecue sauce

1.35kg yellow onions, cut in several large pieces
3 green peppers, seeded, cut into several large pieces
1 bunch celery, cut into large lengths
leaves from 1 bunch of fresh parsley
1 bunch spring onion tops
1 head garlic, separated into cloves and peeled
1.8 litres vegetable oil
675g canned tomato sauce
175ml bottled ketchup
300ml Worcestershire sauce
3 tbsp yellow mustard
3 tbsp sugar
3 tbsp salt
100g unsalted butter
115ml Tabasco sauce

• Place the onions, peppers, celery, parsley, spring onions, and garlic in a food processor until finely chopped.
• Combine the chopped vegetables with the oil, tomato sauce, ketchup, Worcestershire sauce, mustard, sugar, salt, butter and Tabasco in a large heavy pot and stir to mix.
• Cook, stirring often, over a low heat for about 1½ hours.
• Remove from the heat and let cool, skim the oil that rises to the surface and reserve.
• Store the sauce and the oil in airtight containers for up to 2 days in the refrigerator, or in the freezer for up to 3 months.
• Reheat before using.

My barbecue sauce

25g lard or 25ml vegetable oil
1 onion, roughly chopped
1 garlic clove, crushed
1 tsp paprika
200ml tomato ketchup (see left)
150ml tomato juice
45ml Worcestershire sauce
2 tbsp black treacle
1 tbsp cider or white wine vinegar
2 tsp Dijon mustard
1 tsp hot pepper sauce or Tabasco

• Heat the lard or oil in a pan and, when hot, add the onion and garlic and cook for 5 minutes until soft and tender.
• Add the paprika and cook for a further 2 minutes.
• Add the remaining ingredients and bring to the boil; reduce the heat and cook for 30 minutes until reduced and thickened in consistency.
• Remove and allow to cool ready for use.

Green pesto

Olive mayo

Green harissa mayo

Green pesto

100g fresh basil leaves
40g finely grated Parmigiano Reggiano cheese
2 tbsp pine nuts
2 garlic cloves, peeled
20ml extra-virgin olive oil
salt and freshly ground black pepper

• Place the basil, Parmesan, pine nuts and garlic in a liquidiser or food processor and whiz until almost a paste.
• While the motor is running, slowly add the oil through the feed tube at the top, until the pesto sauce is thick and slightly coarse in texture. Season to taste, ready for use.

Tomato and olive pesto

2 garlic cloves, peeled
12 basil leaves
salt and freshly ground black pepper
120g sunblush tomatoes in oil, drained, oil reserved
1 tbsp chopped black olives
1 tbsp grated Parmigiano Reggiano cheese

• Crush the garlic and basil in a mortar and pestle with a little salt until it becomes a paste. Chop the sunblush tomatoes in small pieces and place in a bowl with the olives and Parmesan.
• Add the crushed garlic and basil and mix well.
• Add enough of the reserved tomato oil to form a thick paste around the tomatoes, season to taste and serve.

Basic mayonnaise *makes 300ml*

Some store-bought mayonnaise is fine, but nothing can compare to a home made version. Although taking a few minutes longer, making it really does pay dividends.

3 egg yolks
1 tsp Dijon mustard
1 tsp white wine vinegar
salt and freshly ground white pepper
250ml vegetable or salad (non scented) oil
2 tsp lemon juice

• Place the egg yolks, mustard and vinegar in a bowl, add a little salt and pepper.
• Place the bowl on a wet cloth on a flat surface, this will help keep the bowl steady while adding the oil.
• Slowly, whisk in the oil, pouring it in a fine, steady stream from a jug or ladle.
• Whisk continuously until the mayonnaise begins to thicken; by the time all the oil has been added the mayonnaise will be thick in texture.
• Add the lemon juice and adjust the seasoning to personal taste.
• Mayonnaise will keep for 4–5 days in the refrigerator if kept covered.

PG VARIATIONS

using 100ml of the above recipe

CHUTNEY MAYO

Add 100g chopped mango chutney to the basic recipe. Great with chicken or fish burgers, such as tuna or salmon.

CURRY MAYO

Add 1 tbsp good quality curry paste to the basic recipe. Great with all types of burgers, especially chicken, pork and lamb.

SWEET MUSTARD MAYO

Add 1 tbsp brown sugar along with the eggs, mustard and vinegar, finish with 1 tbsp chopped fresh dill. Great with fish burgers.

AIOLI SAUCE

Add 2 large garlic cloves, crushed, to the mustard, egg and vinegar at the beginning of the basic recipe.

SUNDRIED TOMATO AIOLI

Add 10 sundried tomatoes in oil, drained and finely chopped, to the aioli sauce. Great with all manner of burgers and for a dip for vegetables.

HORSERADISH MAYO

Add 1 tbsp freshly grated horseradish, 1 tsp Dijon mustard, along with 2 tbsp chopped fresh dill or flat-leaf parsley to the basic recipe.

WASABI MAYO

Add ¼ tsp wasabi paste (Japanese horseradish), the juice of ½ lime and 1 tbsp light soy sauce to the basic recipe, finish with 2 tbsp chopped fresh coriander.

OLIVE MAYO

Add 2 tbsp pitted and finely chopped black olives, 1 tsp chopped rinsed capers, and 1 small crushed garlic clove to the basic recipe.

CHILLI MAYO

Add 1 tsp deseeded and very finely chopped red chilli to the basic recipe and mix well. You can use green chilli instead of red if you prefer.

GREEN HARISSA MAYO

Place 2 deseeded green chillies, 1 tsp toasted coriander seeds, 1 garlic clove, along with 50g each fresh coriander, mint, flat-leaf parsley, in a blender. Add 50g cooked spinach and whiz to a smooth purée. Add a spoonful of olive oil if necessary. Transfer to a bowl, add the mayonnaise, and chill ready for use.

CAPER–SAFFRON MAYO

Add ¼ tsp fresh saffron to 3 tbsp boiling water in a small pan and boil for 1 minute; remove and leave to stand for 10 minutes. Add the saffron to the mayonnaise along with 20g rinsed and chopped capers.

Red chilli mayonnaise

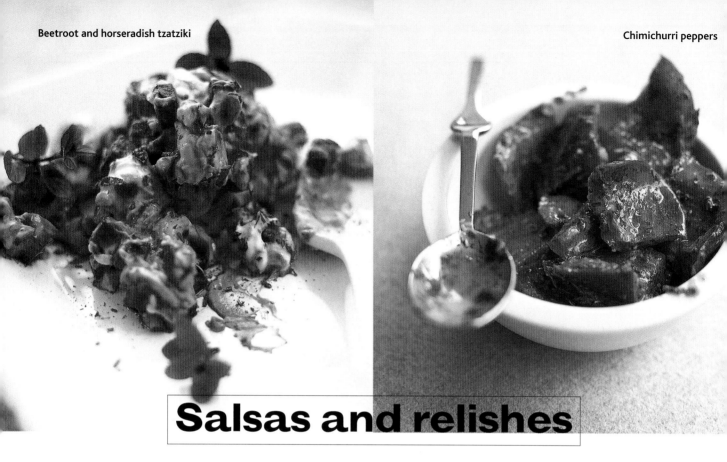

Beetroot and horseradish tzatziki

Chimichurri peppers

Salsas and relishes

Kachumbar piccalilli

Pico de gallo

Beetroot and horseradish tzatziki

⅛ tsp cumin seeds
4 cooked beetroots, peeled
100ml Greek yogurt
2 tbsp chopped fresh mint
1 tbsp horseradish creamed relish
1 tsp lemon juice
salt and freshly ground black pepper

• Heat a dry frying pan over a high heat. Add the cumin seeds and toss gently for 10–20 seconds to give off their fragrance and aromatic smell. Place in a mortar and pestle and crush to a fine powder. Transfer to a bowl.
• Cut the beetroots into 0.5cm dice and add to the cumin. Add the remaining ingredients and season to taste.
• Cover and chill in the refrigerator for 1 hour prior to serving.

Kachumbar piccalilli

juice of 1 lime
2 tbsp tamarind paste
2 tbsp Asian sweet chilli sauce
4 tbsp brown sugar
150ml rice wine vinegar
2.5cm piece root ginger, finely grated
1 tbsp coarse salt
¼ tsp cumin seeds, toasted
¼ tsp coriander seeds, toasted
⅛ tsp turmeric
1 tsp cornflour
400g firm tomatoes, cut into wedges
4 large shallots, peeled, thickly sliced
1 cucumber, halved lengthways, seeds removed, cut into 0.5cm sticks
2 dill pickles, thickly sliced
freshly ground black pepper

• Combine the lime juice, tamarind, chilli sauce and brown sugar in a pan, add the rice wine vinegar, mix well, and bring to the boil, simmer for 5 minutes.
• Add the ginger, salt and spices, cook for a further 5 minutes.
• Mix the cornflour with 2 tsp cold water, then stir into the cooking liquid, simmer for 1 minute, then add the vegetables.
• Simmer gently for 3–4 minutes or until the vegetables are tender.
• Remove to a bowl and allow to go cold, check the seasoning and serve.

Chimichurri peppers

60ml olive oil
2 garlic cloves, crushed
1 tbsp honey
1 jalepeño chilli, deseeded, finely chopped
4 large red peppers, deseeded, cut into large pieces
30ml white wine vinegar
small bunch coriander, roughly chopped
small bunch flat-leaf parsley, roughly chopped
1 tbsp roughly chopped fresh oregano
salt and freshly ground black pepper

• Heat the olive oil in a frying pan, add the garlic, honey and chilli, and cook over a low heat until softened and slightly caramelised.
• Add the pepper pieces, cover, and cook for 5–6 minutes. Add the vinegar, cover again, and cook for a further 5 minutes.
• Remove the lid and add the herbs; increase the heat and sauté until all the liquid has evaporated, season and serve warm.

Pico de gallo

can be made from red or yellow tomatoes

150g red or yellow tomatoes, deseeded, cut into 1cm dice
4 red radishes
1 bunch spring onions, finely chopped
1 yellow pepper, deseeded, cut into 1cm dice
1 jalapeño chilli, deseeded, thinly sliced
2 tbsp chopped fresh coriander
juice of 2 limes
1 garlic clove, crushed

• Combine all the ingredients in a bowl, leave to marinate at room temperature for 3–4 hours to meld the flavours. Kept covered in the refrigerator, it will keep for a day or two, but it is better to make it as needed, when it is fresh and crisp in flavour and texture.

Cooked tomato relish

1 tbsp olive oil
2 shallots, finely chopped
1 garlic clove, crushed
50g brown sugar
2 tbsp white wine vinegar
500g ripe but firm plum tomatoes, blanched, peeled, seeded, cut into 1cm dice
2 tbsp tomato ketchup
1 tbsp cornflour
¼ tsp ground cumin
1 tsp Dijon mustard
salt and freshly ground black pepper

• Heat the olive oil in a pan, add the shallots and garlic and cook for 3–4 minutes until soft but with no colour. Add the sugar and vinegar and stir in until the sugar is dissolved.
• Bring to the boil and cook for 2 minutes. Combine the tomatoes, tomato ketchup, cornflour and cumin and add to the pan; reduce the heat and simmer for 15–20 minutes until thickened to a relish consistency. Remove and allow to cool before adding the mustard and salt and pepper to taste.
• Kept well covered this relish will keep in the refrigerator for up to 2 weeks.

PG VARIATIONS

SPICY TOMATO RELISH
Add 2 small deseeded and chopped red chillies to the shallots and garlic at the beginning of the recipe (or 1 tsp harissa).

GREEK TOMATO RELISH
Add 2 tbsp Greek yogurt, along with 2 tbsp each chopped fresh mint and chopped fresh coriander to the finished relish.

Calypso mojo

75g dried black beans, soaked overnight
25g frozen sweetcorn kernels, defrosted
1 small mango, peeled, cut into 0.5cm dice
2 tbsp maple syrup
2 tbsp chopped fresh mint
1 tbsp olive oil
½ small red onion, thinly sliced
½ garlic clove, crushed
juice of 1 lime

• Drain the beans, place in a pan, cover with water, and boil for 40–50 minutes or until soft; drain and allow to go cold.
• Place the beans in a bowl, stir in the remaining ingredients, and leave to infuse for 30 minutes before using.

Asian guacamole

2 tbsp olive oil
1 small red onion, finely shredded
½ tsp mild curry powder
2 avocados
6 spring onions, finely chopped
1 hot green chilli
juice of 2 limes
handful of coriander leaves
1 tbsp sour cream

• Heat the olive oil in a pan, add the red onion, and cook for 1 minute. Add the curry powder, cook for 2 minutes, allow to go cold.
• Cut the avocados in half, remove the skins and stones.
• Place the avocados in a blender, add the remaining ingredients except the sour cream plus the spiced onion mix. Whiz into a coarse purée, then fold in the sour cream.
• Place in a bowl and refrigerate to allow the flavours to marinate for 1 hour.

Smoky tomato and pepper relish

3 red peppers, halved, deseeded
60ml olive oil
1 red onion, peeled, finely chopped
2 garlic cloves, crushed
½ small red chilli, deseeded, finely chopped
1 tsp smoked paprika
¼ tsp ground cumin
450g tomatoes, blanched, peeled, deseeded and finely chopped
1 tbsp tomato purée
2 tbsp light brown sugar
2 tbsp balsamic vinegar

• Brush the pepper halves with a little of the olive oil, place on a grill pan and place under a preheated grill for 5–8 minutes until charred. Place in a bowl, cover tightly with clingfilm and leave to steam for 5 minutes; peel off the skins and finely chop the peppers.
• Heat 1 tbsp of the oil in a pan, add the red onion, garlic and chilli, and cook for 3–4 minutes until softened. Add the spices, cook for a further minute.
• Add the tomatoes, tomato purée, sugar and vinegar and bring to the boil.
• Add the peppers, reduce the heat, and cook for 20–25 minutes until reduced and thick in consistency.
• Remove from the heat and allow to cool; transfer to a bowl and serve cold.

Balsamic onion pickle

100g dark soft brown sugar
4 large onions, finely chopped
2 Granny Smith apples, peeled, cored and chopped
100ml balsamic vinegar
1 small red pepper, halved, deseeded, finely chopped
1 tsp mustard powder

• In a saucepan place the sugar and 150ml water and, over a low heat, slowly bring to the boil until the sugar dissolves.
• Add the onions, apples, balsamic vinegar, chopped pepper and mustard powder, simmer gently for 1–1½ hours until the mixture becomes thick in consistency and the onions very soft and caramelised.
• Pour into a small, sterilised preserving or jam jar, cover with waxed paper and seal. Leave for 1–2 weeks before using.

Fresh tomato salsa

6 tomatoes, deseeded, chopped
1 small red onion, peeled, chopped
1 small green chilli, deseeded, finely chopped
2 tbsp freshly ground coriander
2 tbsp freshly squeezed lime juice
2 tbsp maple syrup
2 tbsp tomato ketchup (optional)
1 tsp balsamic vinegar
salt and freshly ground black pepper

• Combine all the ingredients together in a bowl, mix thoroughly, then season to taste with salt and pepper. Set aside until ready for use to let the flavours meld together.

PG VARIATIONS

SWEETCORN AND CUCUMBER SALSA
Add 1 small can (200g) sweetcorn, drained, along with 75g deseeded and chopped cucumber to the basic salsa recipe.

ASIAN TOMATO SALSA
Replace the red onion with 4 finely chopped spring onions, plus 2.5cm finely grated root ginger, the balsamic vinegar with rice wine vinegar. Finally add 1 tbsp fish sauce (nam pla).

MANGO SALSA
Add 1 pitted and chopped mango to the Asian tomato salsa variation.

CUBAN AVOCADO SALSA
Mix together 1 peeled, stoned avocado, diced, 2 tbsp chopped fresh coriander, 100g diced fresh pineapple, 1 small chopped red onion, juice of 2 limes, 60ml olive oil, and 2 tbsp maple syrup. Leave for the flavours to meld.

GREEN TOMATO SALSA
Replace the tomatoes with green tomatoes, add 1 crushed garlic clove and a further 2 tbsp chopped fresh coriander

Spicy cranberry–green peppercorn relish

175g cranberries
90g sugar
1 Granny Smith apple, peeled, grated
60ml orange juice
1 tsp green peppercorns, drained, rinsed
1 tbsp white wine vinegar

• Place all the ingredients in a small pan with 150ml water.
• Bring to the boil slowly, then simmer until thick and of jam like consistency. Leave to cool before use. May be kept covered in the refrigerator for up to 10 days.

Mango–coconut cream sauce

100g fresh coriander leaves
75ml unsweetened coconut cream
3 tbsp chopped fresh mint
2 small red chillies, deseeded, finely chopped
2.5cm piece root ginger, finely grated
1 tsp freshly chopped pickled ginger
1 garlic clove, crushed
2 tbsp lime juice
2 tsp brown sugar
1 tsp ground coriander
1 mango, peeled, chopped

• Place the fresh coriander, coconut cream, mint, chillies, gingers, garlic, lime juice, sugar and ground coriander in a blender and whiz to a smooth purée.
• Transfer to a bowl, stir in the chopped mango.

Corn and grilled pineapple mojo

vegetable or sunflower oil for cooking
2 slices fresh pineapple
¼ red pepper, deseeded
50g sweetcorn kernels
1 garlic clove, crushed
juice of 1 lime
2 tbsp chopped fresh mint
1 tbsp caster sugar
1 tbsp honey
salt and freshly ground black pepper

• Preheat a grill pan to very hot, brush with a little oil. Chargrill the pineapple and pepper until lightly charred. Peel the pepper, cut in 1cm dice. Cut the pineapple into small chunks. Place both in a bowl, add remaining ingredients and season to taste

Tomato chutney

400ml cider vinegar
200g sugar
3 garlic cloves, crushed
2.5cm piece root ginger, peeled, finely grated
1½ tsp cayenne pepper
½ tsp ground cinnamon
1.5kg firm ripe plum tomatoes, peeled, cut into large dice
2 Granny Smith apples, peeled, cored and chopped
100g golden raisins

• Place the vinegar, sugar, garlic and ginger and spices in a large pan, slowly bring the contents to the boil, stirring regularly until the sugar has dissolved.
• Lower the heat, add the tomatoes and apples, and cook over a low heat for 30 minutes to 1 hour, depending on the water content of the tomatoes. The tomatoes should remain chunky in texture.
• Add the raisins and cook for a further 10–15 minutes. Cool before use; keep refrigerated until ready for use.

Caesar salad

Coleslaw

There are as many recipes for traditional coleslaw as there are cooks who prepare it. Although coleslaw is generally made with mayonnaise, it is sometimes bound with French dressing or sour cream, which makes a welcome change.

300g white cabbage
150g carrots, peeled
1 onion, peeled
2 green peppers, halved, deseeded
300ml good quality mayonnaise
salt and freshly ground black pepper
pinch of celery salt (optional)

• Remove the outer leaves from the cabbage, cut it into 5cm wedges, remove and discard centre core.
• Using a sharp knife, finely shred it into strips or use the shredding attachment of a food processor.
• Place the shredded cabbage in cold iced water for 30 minutes.
• Meanwhile, cut the carrots into shreds, using a knife or small kitchen mandolin. Thinly shred the onion and green peppers.
• Remove the cabbage from the water and drain it well. Dry it in a clean cloth.
• Place all the ingredients together in a bowl, bind with the mayonnaise, season to taste and chill until required.

PG VARIATIONS

BARBECUE COLESLAW

Add 2 tbsp fresh tomato ketchup and 1 tbsp hot pepper sauce to the basic recipe.

BLUE-CHEESE COLESLAW

Replace the white cabbage with red cabbage, bind with 2 tbsp sour cream instead of mayonnaise, and add 75g crumbled Roquefort cheese to the basic recipe.

RUBY SLAW

Replace the white cabbage with red cabbage, the onion with red onion. Replace the peppers and carrots with 2 shredded cooked beetroots and 2 shredded, cored red apples. Bind with French dressing and sprinkle with 2 tbsp snipped chives.

DELI COLESLAW

Replace the peppers with 5g shredded truffles and add 2 tbsp truffle oil to the mayonnaise base.

Celeriac rémoulade

1 celeriac, peeled, cut into matchsticks
120ml good quality mayonnaise
2 tbsp mixed chopped fresh herbs
½ tsp Dijon mustard
⅛ tsp anchovy essence (optional)
salt and freshly ground black pepper

• Mix all the ingredients together in a bowl, season to taste.

Bacon, spinach and red onion salad

30ml olive oil
4 rashers back bacon
60ml French dressing (vinaigrette)
75g young spinach leaves
1 red onion, peeled, thinly sliced

• Heat a thin film of oil in a frying pan, add the bacon and, over a high heat, cook until very crispy. Add the vinaigrette to the bacon and remove.
• Place the spinach leaves and red onion in a bowl, pour over the hot bacon vinaigrette and toss well.

Pistachio, beetroot and feta tabbouleh

150g cracked wheat
juice of 1 lemon
60ml olive oil
2 cooked beetroots, cut into small wedges
1 red onion, finely chopped
4 red radishes, sliced
2 tbsp chopped fresh mint
salt and freshly ground black pepper
75g feta cheese, cut into 1cm cubes
45g peeled pistachios

• Place the cracked wheat in a bowl, cover with boiling water and leave for 15–20 minutes; drain well and dry in a cloth. Place in a clean bowl, add the lemon juice, oil, beetroot, onion, radishes and mint; mix well and season to taste.
• Dress on the serving dish, scatter the feta and pistachios over before serving.

Creole rémoulade slaw

60ml good quality mayonnaise
1 tsp Creole mustard
1 hard-boiled egg, chopped
1 tbsp chopped fresh flat-leaf parsley
salt and freshly ground black pepper
pinch of cayenne
75g napa cabbage (Chinese cabbage), shredded
2 shallots, peeled, halved, thinly sliced
2 sticks celery, peeled, thinly sliced
1 red pepper, halved, deseeded, thinly sliced
1 anchovy fillet, rinsed, chopped

• In a bowl combine the mayonnaise with the mustard, egg and parsley and season to taste.
• Add the vegetables and anchovy, toss together to bind and check the seasoning.

Caesar salad

1 egg yolk
2 garlic cloves, crushed
30ml white wine vinegar
2 anchovy fillets
1 tsp Worcestershire sauce
½ tsp Dijon mustard
salt and freshly ground black pepper
125ml light olive oil
60ml olive oil or melted butter
100g rustic country bread, cut into 1cm dice
2 heads romaine lettuce, inner leaves only
75g freshly shaved Parmigiano Reggiano

• Make the dressing: place the egg yolk, garlic, vinegar, anchovies, Worcestershire sauce, mustard, and a little salt and pepper in a blender, and whiz until smooth. With the motor running, gradually add the light olive oil through the feed tube.
• Heat the olive oil or butter in a frying pan, add the bread and cook over a gentle heat until golden and crispy. Remove from the pan and allow to cool.
• Separate the romaine leaves, wash and dry them, then tear into fairly large pieces. Place in a bowl and toss with the dressing. Scatter the croutons over and sprinkle the shaved Parmesan on top.

Breads

Burger bap with black sesame seeds

Basic burger bap recipe

(makes 8)

When making these baps, I recommend using a small food processor with a dough hook, which helps aerate the mix better and gives a more satisfying result. But preparing by hand is fine.

575g strong flour
½ tsp salt
½ tsp sugar
25g unsalted butter, softened
25g fresh yeast
sunflower oil for greasing
25g plain or black sesame seeds (optional)
1 egg beaten with 15ml milk

• Into a large bowl, sift the flour, salt and sugar. Add the butter and blend well together.
• Place the yeast in a small bowl, add 365ml water and leave the liquid to become bubbly, about 10–15 minutes.
• Add the yeast liquid to the flour and beat well for 7–8 minutes to amalgamate the dough.
• Cover the dough with a warm damp cloth and place in a warm area for up to 1 hour to prove.
• Lightly grease a large baking tray.
• Divide the dough into 8 large balls or baps. Arrange the baps spaced well apart to allow for expansion as they cook; if using, sprinkle the sesame seeds over the surface of the baps.
• Cover again with the damp cloth, allow to prove again for 45 minutes.
• Preheat the oven to 220°C/Gas 7.
• Brush the top of each bap with the egg and milk glaze and place in the oven for 30–35 minutes. Remove the baps and leave to rest for 20 minutes before using.

PG VARIATIONS

ONION AND THYME BAPS
Sauté 1 finely chopped onion and 1 tsp picked thyme together in 10g butter until soft, then add to the dough during the last minute of beating.

CHORIZO BAPS
Add 200g finely diced chorizo or bacon to the dough during the last minute of beating.

CHEESE BAPS
Add 175g grated Cheddar cheese, along with the butter at the beginning.

English muffins

(makes 10)

450g strong bread flour
10g salt
7g easy blend yeast
½ tsp sugar
200ml warm water
140ml warm milk
flour for dusting

• Place the flour and salt in a large mixing bowl, add the yeast and make a well in the centre.
• Add the sugar to the lukewarm liquids and pour into the well in the flour mixture. Mix with your hands until it forms a soft and slightly sticky dough.
• Turn out the dough on to a floured work surface and knead with floured hands for 10 minutes until it is soft, elastic, smooth and no longer sticky.
• Return the dough to the bowl, cover with a damp cloth, and leave to rise in a warm place until doubled in size, about 1 hour.
• Turn out the dough on to the work surface and knead for a further 5 minutes. Divide the dough into 10 evenly sized pieces and shape into balls. Drop on to a well dusted baking tray leaving plenty of room to allow for expansion, then sprinkle them with flour.
• Cover the tray of muffins with another lightweight baking tray and leave for 30 minutes or until doubled in size again.
• Heat a heavy cast iron frying pan or griddle until moderately hot and cook them, a few at a time, turning them as you place them on the pan. Cook them slowly for 10–12 minutes on each side, until golden brown, turning them with a palette knife during cooking. They are cooked when the surface springs back when pressed.
• Remove the muffins from the pan and leave to cool on a rack ready for use.

Pitta bread

(makes 8 large or 12 mini pitta breads)
These Arabic-style flatbreads are great for holding kebabs or small burgers. Ensure you have your oven set at the highest possible setting for the best result.

25g fresh yeast
pinch of sugar
400ml warm water
450g plain flour plus extra for dusting
½ tsp salt
sunflower oil for greasing

• In a bowl, mix the yeast with the sugar and 4 tbsp of the water; leave the liquid to become bubbly, about 10–15 minutes. Mix the flour and salt in a mixing bowl, make a well in the centre and add the yeast mixture. Work into a dough with the remaining water to a firm consistency. Knead for 10 minutes.
• When the dough is smooth and pliable, shape into a ball, place in a lightly greased bowl and cover with clingfilm or a damp cloth. Set aside in a warm place for 1–1½ hours or until doubled in size.
• Preheat the oven to 260°C/Gas 9 or highest setting. Turn out the dough on to a floured surface. Punch down the dough, then divide into 8 or 12 equal portions. Roll each portion into a ball, dust with flour and place on a board. Cover with a dry cloth and prove for a further 15 minutes.
• Grease 3 large baking sheets lightly with oil, place in the hot oven for 5 minutes. Roll out each ball of dough on a floured surface with a floured rolling pin to a rough circle (about 15cm diameter for large pittas). Transfer 2 or 3 at a time to a hot baking sheet. Cook in the oven for about 6 minutes until puffed up but still quite pale in colour. Repeat with the remaining pittas, cooking them a few at a time.
• Place on a cooling rack, then cover with a cloth to keep them soft.

Brioche

(makes 2 loaves)

225g unsalted butter at room temperature
3 large eggs
300g strong white bread flour
pinch of salt
7g easy-blend dried yeast
about 2 tbsp warm milk, if needed
flour for dusting
sunflower oil for greasing
1 small egg yolk, lightly beaten with 1 tsp water

• Place the butter in the bowl of a small table top electric mixer, or mixing bowl if using a hand held mixer. Beat until soft and creamy.
• Beat in the eggs one at a time. Sift the flour and salt and add to the bowl with the yeast and beat thoroughly. If the dough seems too dry to come together, add the warmed milk. The dough should be firm at this stage.
• Fit the dough hook to the mixer, or turn out the dough on a lightly floured work surface, knead until smooth and quite elastic.
• Shape into a ball, place in a clean bowl, cover with a cloth and leave at room temperature to rise until doubled in volume.
• On a lightly floured surface, knock back the dough, then shape it into an oblong and place on a lightly oiled loaf tin of 1.3 litre capacity. The dough should half fill the tin. Cover and leave to rise at room temperature until the dough fills the tin.
• Preheat the oven to 190°C / Gas 5.
• Brush the top of the loaf with the egg yolk mixture, then bake for about 30 minutes or until risen and golden brown.
• Test if the bread is done by tipping it out of the tin and tapping it gently on the base, it should sound hollow.
• Turn out on to a wire rack to cool.

PG VARIATIONS

RICHARD CORRIGAN'S BACON BRIOCHE
• Heat a little oil in a frying pan, add 175g rindless streaky bacon, cut into small pieces, and fry until golden. Add 1 finely chopped onion and 1 tsp chopped fresh marjoram, cook until softened, remove and cool.
• Add the mixture to the dough before kneading for the first time.

CHEESE BRIOCHE
Add 100g grated cheese to the dough before kneading for the first time.

Cumin naan bread

(makes 8 naan breads)

1 tsp cumin seeds
250g self raising flour
2 tbsp Greek yogurt
1 tsp salt
125ml warm water
½ tsp ground coriander
flour for dusting

• Heat a small pan over medium heat, add the cumin seeds and dry toast for 20 seconds until they give off an aroma. Remove and allow to cool.
• Place the flour, yogurt and salt in a large bowl, add the warm water, a little at a time, working it into the flour with your fingers to form a sticky dough.
• Mix in the coriander and toasted cumin seeds. Knead for a few seconds then cover with a damp cloth to prove.
• Leave at room temperature for 1–1½ hours.
• Preheat a grill to its highest setting.
• Flour your hands and pull off small pieces of dough, shape them into a ball.
• Roll out each ball on a floured surface to about 15–20cm in diameter.
• Place the now formed naans on grilling trays, place under the grill until they puff up and blister about 50–60 seconds, turn over and repeat on the other side; serve warm.

PG VARIATIONS

By adding different ingredients, you can vary this simple bread:

GARLIC NAAN
Add 2 small crushed garlic cloves to the formed dough.

MUSTARD SEED NAAN
Sprinkle the rolled naan lightly with black mustard seeds before grilling.

COCONUT NAAN
Add 50g dried desiccated coconut to the dough.

Focaccia

(makes 1 loaf)

Focaccia is an Italian-style flatbread made with good quality olive oil. It may be made plain, as in my basic recipe below, or topped with all manner of wonderful toppings. I have included some of my particular favourites.

350g plain flour
½ tsp salt
10g easy-blend dried yeast
250ml warm water
45ml olive oil
flour for dusting
sunflower oil for greasing
1 tsp coarse sea salt
60ml olive oil

• Sift the flour and salt into a large mixing bowl, stir in the yeast, then make a well in the centre of the bowl.
• Pour in the warm water and 30ml of the oil, mix well adding a little more water if the mix seems too dry in texture.
• Turn the dough out onto a lightly floured surface and knead for about 10 minutes until smooth and elastic.
• Return the dough to a greased bowl, cover with a cloth and leave in a warm place for about 1 hour until doubled in size.
• Knock back and knead the dough for 2–3 minutes.
• Preheat the oven to 220°C/Gas 7.
• Roll out the dough about 1cm thick, then transfer to a greased baking sheet or small roasting tin.
• Cover with a cloth again and leave to rise again for 45 minutes.
• Using your fingertips, make indentations into the dough 0.5cm deep.
• Drizzle about half the oil over, sprinkle the sea salt on top, and place in the oven. Bake for 25–30 minutes until golden; brush all over with the remaining olive oil, turn out onto a wire rack and leave to cool slightly before eating.

PG VARIATIONS

• Use flavoured oils, such as herb, saffron or chilli for an interesting change.

Top the focaccia with all manner of wonderful flavours:
• Thinly sliced red onion and chopped rosemary.
• Thinly sliced garlic and pesto.
• Chopped sunblush tomatoes and black olives.

Focaccia

Potatoes

Matchstick fries

Matchstick fries

2 medium-large potatoes
vegetable oil for deep frying
¼ tsp caraway seeds, toasted (optional)
½ tsp coarse sea salt

• Peel the potatoes, then using a Japanese vegetable mandolin, cut them into julienne strips. Wash in cold water to remove the starch.
• Dry in a clean cloth.
• Heat the oil until 180°C, add the potatoes and fry until golden and crispy.
• Drain on kitchen paper.
• Place the caraway seeds and salt in a mortar and pestle and crush until fine then sprinkle over the crispy fried potatoes.
• Serve hot or cold.

Oven cheese fries

2 potatoes, well washed
100ml vegetable oil
salt and freshly ground black pepper
25g fresh white breadcrumbs
25g freshly grated Cheddar cheese
50g unsalted butter, melted

• Preheat the oven to 180°C/Gas 4.
• Cut the potatoes into thick wedges, dry well in a cloth and place in a baking tin. Pour the vegetable oil over and toss together well. Season to taste.
• Place in the oven and cook for 25–30 minutes or until golden and crispy.
• In a bowl combine the breadcrumbs, cheese and butter, and sprinkle over the potatoes. Return the potatoes to the oven until the cheese and breadcrumbs are golden and form a light golden crust on top, then serve.

Twice-cooked jacket potatoes

4 baking potatoes, well washed
50g unsalted butter
2 garlic cloves
75g fresh white breadcrumbs
½ tsp Dijon mustard
3 tbsp chopped fresh flat-leaf parsley

• Preheat a grill to its highest setting.
• Prick the potatoes all over with a small knife, place in a microwave for 6–8 minutes or until cooked.
• Cut the potatoes in half crossways and stand cut side up on a grill pan.
• Heat a frying pan until hot, add the butter, garlic and parsley and cook until the butter begins to foam up. Add the breadcrumbs, mustard and cook for 1 minute.
• Spoon the fried crumbs over the potatoes and place them under the grill to grill to a golden colour, remove and serve.

The ultimate fries

4 large floury potatoes
vegetable or sunflower oil for deep frying
coarse sea salt

• Peel the potatoes, rinse under cold water, then dry in a clean cloth or kitchen paper. Cut into strips about 1cm wide by 5–7cm.
• Half fill a deep fat fryer or deep, heavy based saucepan with the oil and heat it to 150°C .
• Fry the potatoes in the oil in batches for 5–8 minutes until they are soft but still very pale in colour. Lift out with a slotted spoon and drain on kitchen paper. The chips can be prepared up to this stage several hours in advance, as long as the final frying is done just before serving.
• Raise the temperature of the oil to 200°C and return the fries to the oil in batches.
• Fry for 2–3 minutes until golden and crisp. Remove with a slotted spoon.
• Drain the fries on kitchen paper, then serve sprinkled liberally with the coarse salt.

PG VARIATIONS

• Season the fries with a cumin and paprika salt mix, made by mixing together 1 tsp ground cumin, ¼ tsp smoked paprika, 2 tbsp coarse salt and a pinch of sugar.
• Pass the cooked fries through 50g unsalted butter, melted, and mixed with 2 tbsp chopped fresh flat-leaf parsley and 2 crushed garlic cloves.
• Place the cooked fries in a dish, sprinkle with Cheddar cheese and set under a preheated hot grill until the cheese is bubbling and golden.

Potato salad

300g small new potatoes, scrubbed, halved
5 tbsp vegetable oil
30ml white wine vinegar
1 tsp German mustard
1 tsp caster sugar
salt and freshly ground black pepper
150ml hot chicken stock
8 cherry tomatoes, halved
2 sweet dill pickled gherkins, thinly sliced
2 shallots, peeled, cut into thin rings
2 spring onions, shredded
1 tbsp chopped fresh chives

• Boil the potatoes in a pan of salted water until tender, drain well and set aside.
• In a bowl, whisk the oil, vinegar, mustard, sugar and a little seasoning together.
• Add the chicken stock, mix together, then pour over the hot potatoes. Cover with a lid and leave to cool to room temperature, by which time the potatoes will have absorbed all the flavours.
• Transfer to a bowl and add the remaining ingredients; adjust seasoning to taste and serve (do not refrigerate or all the flavours will be lost).

Patatas con ajo

500g potatoes, cut into large chunks
125ml olive oil
2 garlic cloves, crushed
salt
pinch of paprika

• Cook the potatoes in boiling, salted water until tender. Drain, saving a little of the cooking water.
• Mash the potatoes, adding a little of the reserved cooking water to make a smooth purée.
• Mix the oil, garlic and salt and stir into the hot mash. Serve sprinkled with a little paprika.

Vegetables

Sweet potato fries

4 large sweet potatoes
vegetable or sunflower oil for deep frying
salt and freshly ground black pepper

• Peel the sweet potatoes, rinse them, and cut into strips, lengthways, about 1cm thick. Pat with a clean cloth or kitchen paper to dry.
• Half fill a deep fat fryer or deep, heavy based saucepan with the oil and heat it to 190°C.
• Fry the sweet potatoes in the oil in batches for 3–4 minutes until golden. Drain on kitchen paper, season and serve.

Tempura sweet potatoes

2 red sweet potatoes, peeled
½ tsp ground ginger
½ tsp ground coriander
½ tsp ground cumin
small pinch of dried chilli powder
100g plain flour
salt and freshly ground black pepper
200ml iced soda water
1 small egg white, lightly beaten
vegetable oil for deep frying

• Thinly slice the sweet potatoes on a kitchen mandolin about 0.5cm thick, place in a bowl.
• Add the spices, mix well, and leave to marinate for 1 hour.
• Whisk the flour, salt and pepper in a bowl with the iced soda water and egg white; whisk until just blended, do not overmix. Chill for 1 hour.
• Heat a deep fat fryer or large saucepan with sufficient oil. Working in batches, dip the potato slices into the batter then drop into the hot oil.
• Fry until golden, remove with a slotted spoon, and drain on kitchen paper; serve hot.

Spicy red-chilli onion rings

2 large onions, peeled, cut into 0.5cm thick
  slices, separated into rings
120ml buttermilk or whole milk
2 tbsp plain flour
1 tbsp cornflour
1 tbsp red chilli powder
1 tsp ground cumin
1 tsp smoked paprika
½ tsp garlic powder
salt
pinch of sugar
vegetable oil for deep frying

• Place the onions in a bowl, pour the milk over, and leave to stand for 30 minutes.
• In a large bowl, mix together the flour, cornflour, spices and garlic powder, along with a little salt and sugar.
• Half fill a deep fat fryer or deep, heavy based saucepan with the oil and heat it to 180°C.
• Taking a few onion rings at a time, remove them from the milk, then dip them into the flour coating.
• Fry until golden, remove and drain on kitchen paper, and serve.

Fire-roasted vegetables

2 aubergine, cut into 1cm wedges
2 courgettes, cut into 1cm slices
1 red pepper, halved, deseeded, cut into
  2.5cm dice
1 green pepper, halved, deseeded, cut into
  2.5cm dice
1 red onion, halved, cut into thick wedges
90ml olive oil
1 garlic clove, crushed
2 tsp balsamic vinegar
salt and freshly ground black pepper
oregano leaves to garnish

• Place the cut vegetables in a large bowl.
• Mix the olive oil, garlic and vinegar and pour over the vegetables, season, then toss together. Leave to marinate for 1 hour.
• Thread the vegetables onto 8 pre-soaked wooden skewers, with an eye to colour.
• Heat a chargrill until hot, add the skewers and chargrill for 4–5 minutes, turning them regularly until cooked.
• Remove and serve sprinkled with oregano leaves.

Spicy plantain chips (chilli willies)

2 large green plantains
vegetable oil for deep frying
coarse sea salt
large pinch of chilli powder

• Green plantains can be difficult to peel– here is how you do it. Fill a sink with warm-hottish water. Cut the ends off the plantains, make 3–4 slits lengthways through the skin, then leave to soak in the water for 20–25 minutes. Once soaked you can easily peel them by running your fingers under the skin. Slice the plaintains 0.3cm thick.
• Half fill a deep fat fryer or deep, heavy based saucepan with the oil and heat it to 180°C.
• Drop the plantain slices, a few at a time, into the oil and fry until golden and crisp. Drain on kitchen paper; season with salt and a touch of chilli powder, toss gently and serve.

Chickpea fries

300g chickpea flour (gram flour)
1 garlic clove, crushed
salt and freshly ground black pepper
olive oil for greasing
vegetable oil for deep frying

• Place the chickpea flour and garlic in a pan with a little salt and pepper. Whisk in 700ml water to form a smooth paste.
• Place on a low–medium heat, whisking continuously until very thick, about 5 minutes. Then beat with a wooden spoon until completely smooth.
• Lightly grease a small loaf tin with the olive oil. Transfer the chickpea mix into the tin and smooth off the surface with a wet knife.
• Cover the tin with foil and place in the refrigerator overnight.
• Unmould the terrine onto a cutting board, then cut into 1cm thick slices, then cut each slice into 0.5cm strips to form thin chips.
• Half fill a deep fat fryer or deep, heavy based saucepan with the oil and heat it to 180°C.
• Working in small batches, fry the chips until golden.
• Remove with a slotted spoon onto kitchen paper, lightly season with salt and serve.

Spicy plantain chips (chilli willies)

Index

Acknowledgements

Author

I gratefully thank and acknowledge the assistance of the following people, wonderful individuals, without whose support this book would not have been possible.

To Jacqui and Kate at Jacqui Small Publishers for inspiring me to write this book, thank you for your friendship and encouragement.

Linda Tubby, Gus Filgate and Lawrence Morton for their individual artistic skills.

Madeline Weston and Jane Middleton who helped turn my aspirations into print.

My personal assistant Lara King for just organising me!

Ryan Stevenson, my assistant pastry chef, for never complaining when I asked for yet another batch of baps, breads or focaccia for photo shoots ... great job, and Danilo Sita for helping with the recipe preparation.

To all my family, and my agents, for their continued support and enthusiasm with my writing.

Guest Recipes

I would like to thank the following select chefs, writers and friends, for whom I hold the utmost admiration, for graciously supplying their favourite burger recipes for inclusion in this book (in order of appearance):

Mark McEwan, Eula Mae Doré, Chris Galvin, Richard Corrigan, Anthony Worrall Thompson, Jill Dupleix, Andrew Blake, Marcus Samuelsson, Peter Gordon.